CHOPIN'S
MUSICAL STYLE

CHOPIN'S MUSICAL STYLE

BY

GERALD ABRAHAM

LONDON
OXFORD UNIVERSITY PRESS
NEW YORK TORONTO

Oxford University Press, Ely House, London W. 1

GLASGOW   NEW YORK   TORONTO   MELBOURNE   WELLINGTON
CAPE TOWN   IBADAN   NAIROBI   DAR ES SALAAM   LUSAKA   ADDIS ABABA
DELHI   BOMBAY   CALCUTTA   MADRAS   KARACHI   LAHORE   DACCA
KUALA LUMPUR   SINGAPORE   HONG KONG   TOKYO

ISBN 0 19 315309 2

First edition 1939
Sixth impression 1973

Printed in Great Britain

CONTENTS

INTRODUCTION

THIS little book is an attempt to show the gradual unfolding and maturing of Chopin's musical mind, to investigate the working of that mind, and to isolate and define those qualities which make Chopin's work unique in the history of music. Every one admits Chopin's charm (though some may find it not to their taste), but it is probable that comparatively few understand precisely how he worked his miracles.

But, it may be asked, is it of any use to the practical musician, particularly to the pianist, to know this? Emphatically, yes. It is becoming more and more generally recognized that intelligent interpretation is practically impossible without thorough knowledge of a composer's style. That is true of all composers in some degree, and particularly true of Chopin. To take one example: more than sixty years ago Sir Henry Hadow[1] wrote: 'In the twelfth bar of the well-known Nocturne in E flat (Op. 9, No. 2), there is a connecting passage which, when we see it on paper, seems to consist of a rapid series of remote and recondite modulations. *When we hear it played in the manner which Chopin intended* [my italics] we feel that there is only one real modulation, and that the rest of the passage is an iridescent play of colour, an effect of superficies, not an effect of substance.' Without real understanding of

[1] *Studies in Modern Music* (Second Series). Seeley, Service & Co., Ltd., 1894.

Chopin's style, it is impossible to distinguish between 'effects of superficies' and 'effects of substance', and hence to play them as they were intended to be played. To put it in another way: the passage is a harmonic parenthesis—and the parenthetic effect must be conveyed by the player.

And such parentheses occur not only in the harmony, but in the formal structure. Writing of the E major Scherzo, Op. 54, Hugo Leichtentritt[1] draws attention to the eight-bar 'asides' (bars 25–32, 57–64, etc.) which his analysis shows to be inserted in the main argument, and which 'should be different in tone-colour from the real melody-bearing matter. They should be played incidentally as it were—less emphatically than the main melodic line'. Intelligent analysis is one of the interpreter's most valuable tools.

This book should also be of help to the student of harmony. For, as is now generally admitted, Chopin's chromaticism marks a stage of the greatest importance in the evolution of the harmonic language. He is the forerunner of Liszt and Wagner, and hence of the modern atonalists, the first composer seriously to undermine the solid system of diatonic tonalism created by the Viennese classical masters and their contemporaries in other countries.

Writing for the practical musician, I have left almost untouched two problems of great interest to the musicologist: the origins of Chopin's musical style, and the true chronological order of his compositions.

[1] *Analyse der Chopin'sche Klavierwerke*. Berlin. 1922.

It is fairly obvious that the young Chopin was musically descended from Hummel and Field and Moscheles rather than from Mozart, whom he adored, and Beethoven, whom he seems to have known imperfectly and admired but moderately. There are traces here and there of a slight Weberian strain. But what of Schubert? 'I think Chopin knew too little of his music to be appreciably influenced by him', says Niecks.[1] 'At any rate, I fail to perceive how and where the influence reveals itself.' Yet they have certain traits in common, though whether Chopin acquired them from Schubert or from the circumambient musical atmosphere is a matter for debate—or, rather, for investigation. Again, there is the influence of Spohr, whom we know Chopin did admire (see his letters of October 3, 1829, and September 18, 1830). Was Chopin's chromatic harmony influenced by Spohr's? And if so, to what extent?

And what of the influence of Joseph Elsner (1769–1854), the Silesian-born musician who had the honour of being Chopin's only composition teacher? Elsner's innumerable compositions in every genre, from opera and symphony to the small piano piece, are generally inaccessible. But, according to Niecks, 'most accounts agree in stating that he wrote in the style of the modern Italians, that is to say, what were called the modern Italians in the later part of the last and the earlier part of this century'. 'Elsner's productions are in the style

[1] *Frederick Chopin as a Man and Musician.* Novello. 1888. (Third edition, 1902.)

of Paër and Mayer's music', says Fétis. According
to Dr. Maria Ottich, his twenty-eight polonaises
'anticipate in certain traits the great perfector of
this form'. And the author of the article 'Elsner'
in Schilling's *Universal-Lexikon der Tonkunst*[1] remarks that 'one forgives him readily [in consideration of the general excellence of his style] the
offences against the law of harmonic connexion that
occur here and there, and the facility with which he
sometimes disregards the fixed rules of strict part-
writing'. It is inconceivable that Chopin was quite
uninfluenced by his master. But how great was the
influence? In what direction? Are Chopin's own
'offences against the law of harmonic connexion' (as
then administered) reflections of Elsner's?

These are questions which I have not attempted
to answer, though to do so would be a fascinating
task. But from the point of view of the working
musician of to-day the music of Hummel and Spohr
and Moscheles—to say nothing of Elsner—is un-
happily as dead as the men who wrote it, and
Field's nearly so, while Chopin's is gloriously alive.
Moreover, no matter how much Chopin may have
been indebted to these others in his caterpillar-
and-chrysalis stage, by the time he emerged at
twenty-one as the lovely chatoyant butterfly we
think of as the true Chopin, he was as free from
debt to predecessors as any composer in the whole
history of music. I have confined myself here to
tracing the evolution of the butterfly from the
caterpillar without bothering unduly about the

[1] Quoted by Niecks.

origin of the eggs from which the caterpillar emerged.

I have concernèd myself with chronology only so far as to divide Chopin's output into three main periods: the positively and comparatively immature works written before his arrival in Paris in September, 1831; the works of 1831–40; and the compositions of the last nine years. (A number of works have been re-dated in the light of Mr. Arthur Hedley's list in the fifth edition of *Grove*.)

This practice of drawing lines at the end of a creative artist's 'periods' is as unavoidable as it is detestable.[1] And in this case the lines are drawn less arbitrarily than may appear at first sight. No one will deny that the boyish compositions of 1822–8 are immature. And though, as Niecks says, 'at the very first glance it becomes evident that the works of the last two years (1829–31) are decidedly superior to those he wrote before that time', they hardly belong—except the first set of Etudes, Op. 10—to the true Chopin canon. Chopin did not fully become himself till his arrival in Paris.

The division between the works of the second and third periods is much less clearly defined and less easy to justify. Nevertheless, while many of the third-period compositions are hardly distinguish-

[1] 'It would be easy to classify the Polish master's works according to three or even four successive styles, but I have no taste for this cheap kind of useless ingenuity', says Niecks. But such classification if cheap is certainly not useless; on the contrary, it is a valuable convenience.

able from those of the second, I hope to be able to
show that in his last nine years Chopin produced a
number of works more powerfully conceived, more
organically constructed (at the risk of being mis-
understood, I am tempted to say 'more symphonic'),
than any he had written before. They also show a
new tendency to polyphony: and a slight—a very
slight—pretext for drawing the line just here is
provided by a sentence in a letter to Fontana,
undated but apparently written in July or August,
1841: 'Send without fail Cherubini's *traité*; I think
it's *du contrepoint* (I don't remember the title well)'
(the *Cours de Contrepoint et de la Fugue*, which had
been published in 1835).

In my choice of music-type examples, I have
worked on the assumption that the reader possesses
copies of Chopin's better-known works, which he
would be well advised to keep at his side. In the
case of lesser-known compositions, I have used
music-type more freely to facilitate reference.

EVOLUTION OF A MUSICAL PERSONALITY

(1822–1831)

THE more important compositions of Chopin's nonage may be divided into two main groups: more or less showy concert-pieces in forms which he abandoned in later life:

Rondeau in C minor, Op. 1 (1825)
Variations sur un air national allemand (Op. posth.) (1826)
Rondeau à la mazurka, Op. 5 (1826)
'La ci darem la mano' de l'opera *Don Juan*. Varie, Op. 2 (1827)[1]
Rondeau pour deux pianos, Op. 73 (1828)
Fantaisie sur des airs polonais, Op. 13 (1828)
Krakowiak, Op. 14 (1828)

and the first essays in those smaller forms which he afterwards practised so sucessfully. With these we may group the youthful C minor Piano Sonata:

Mazurkas in G major and B flat major (1825), in A minor, Op. 68, No. 2 (1827), in D major (1829), in C and F, Op. 68, Nos. 1 and 3 (1829), and Op 6 and 7 (mostly 1830–1)

[1] Not 1828, as Niecks supposed. Chopin mentions the work in letter written towards the end of 1827.

Nocturnes in E minor, Op. 72, No. 1 (1827),
Op. 9, and Op. 15, Nos. 1 and 2 (1830–1)

Polonaises in G sharp minor (1822), D minor,
B flat major and F minor, Op. 71, Nos. 1, 2 and
3 (1827–29)

Sonata in C minor, Op. 4 (1827)

Valses in B minor, Op. 69, No. 2, in D flat,
Op. 70, No. 3, and in E minor (all about
1829)

In addition there are the quite unimportant
Marche funèbre in C minor, Op. 72, No. 2 (1829),
and the Trois Ecossaises (Op. 72, No. 3) (1826).

To these two groups we must add a third consisting
of the most significant 'border-line' works written
during the transition period 1829–31, all important, yet not quite to be classed with the works
of maturity:

Concerto in F minor, Op. 21 (1829)
Concerto in E minor, Op. 11 (1830)
Grand Polonaise brillante, Op. 22 (1830-1)
Douze Grandes Etudes, Op. 10 (1829–32)

Consideration of this third group, however, had
better be postponed till we have looked a little
more closely at the first two.

It will be seen that the earliest generally known
work of Chopin's is the Polonaise in G sharp minor
(No. 14 of the Polish National Edition), the composition of which is commonly attributed to the
year 1822, when the composer was twelve. Niecks

considered that 'on account of the *savoir faire* and invention exhibited in it' this must have been written at 'a considerably later time'. But actually there is little in the work that might not have come from a very talented boy of twelve. Neither the spirit of the piece nor its harmony or structure distinguishes it from hundreds of contemporary brilliant salon-pieces of the same kind. The piano figuration is of the type one finds again and again in Hummel and Weber, the trio being particularly Weberian.

Study of the rather later Variations sur un air national allemand and the first three Rondeaux is more rewarding, though they reveal little of Chopin's true musical individuality. But that does begin to emerge. The finale of the 'German' variations (*tempo di valse*) and the beginning of the D flat episode of the C minor Rondeau already give out a little of the unmistakable Chopinesque ring. One has only to compare the latter:

Ex. 1

with a very similar passage in the *allegretto* of
Hummel's Sonata in A flat:

Ex. 2

to see both how the young Chopin belonged to his
period and how he breathed a new poetic spirit into
familiar forms. The end of the first sixteen-bar
period of the *tempo di valse* of the Variations brings
a formula:

Ex. 3

familiar in the more mature Valses (cf. Op. 34,
No. 1, and Op. 42) and the coda, with its cantabile
motive sung out in the tenor, sounds like a faint
premonition of several passages in the Scherzi,
notably the peroration of the C sharp minor. One
also notes the appearance of one of Chopin's

favourite chords: the diminished seventh on the sharpened fourth[1] (cf. the G sharp minor Polonaise, bar 10; the A minor Mazurka dedicated to Emile Gaillard, bar 2; and later works *passim*). (As we shall soon find, the diminished seventh plays an extremely important part in Chopin's harmony.) And so with other things: widely spread chords here (Op. 1, bars 102–3 and 106–7), a sequence there (*ibid.*, bars 132–5).

These are portents which we see to be portentous only because we know what they portended. But broadly speaking the C minor Rondeau and the Variations on a German Air—and, for that matter, the slightly later but even less interesting Rondeau for two pianos—show Chopin merely at his taking-off point. His thematic material, his harmony, even his piano-writing—the figuration still usually bounded by the limits of the octave-stretch—are exactly what one would expect of a talented young contemporary of Hummel and Moscheles. And, incidentally, a composer who began in those days by imitating Hummel and Moscheles had not chosen bad models. Hummel in particular, though not a great master, was something more than a mere talented imitator of his first teacher, Mozart. It is true his music is often platitudinous and usually rather square-cut. But it has exquisite polish. (Hummel studied not only under Mozart, but

---

[1] In its second inversion, i.e. what old-fashioned English theorists would consider a third inversion of the supertonic minor ninth. Here, as so often later, Chopin employs convenient rather than correct notation: F double sharp instead of G natural.

under Clementi, Albrechtsberger, and Salieri, so it
is hardly surprising that he was a master of the
technique of composition.) If his figuration is often
conventional—as Beethoven's piano-writing often
is, too, for that matter—it sometimes assumes
forms that suggest the mature Chopin himself, as
in these two cases in the Sonata in F sharp minor,
Op. 81:

Ex. 4

And in such passages as these from the B minor
Concerto, Op. 89:

Ex. 5

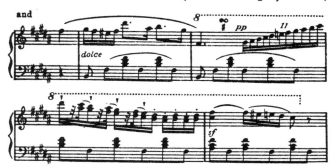

his idyllic romanticism is hardly distinguishable from Field's, and he comes fairly near to the mature Chopin of such Nocturnes as Op. 9, No. 3, and Op. 32, No. 2. He even uses the marking *tempo rubato* in the first movement of his C major Piano Sonata. He is in fact the chief link between Mozart and Chopin.[1]

Hummel's influence is much less apparent in the Rondeau à la mazurka, Op. 5, though, as we shall see, Chopin remained under it at least until 1830, when he wrote the E minor Concerto. But this Opus 5 is much more genuinely Chopinesque than anything that had preceded it. 'Who could fail to recognize him in the peculiar sweet and persuasive flows of sound, and the serpent-like winding of the melodic outline, the widespread chords, the chromatic progressions, the dissolving of the harmonies and the linking of their constituent parts!' cries Niecks. But that which especially

[1] More important even than Field, who was himself indebted to Hummel (cf. Field's Piano Concerto in A flat).

stamps the Rondeau à la mazurka with the mark
of its authorship is—the fact that it is a mazurka.
Here for the first time Chopin shows his intense
love of the idiom of Polish folk music. It is Polish
fresh air that blows away the Hummelian atmosphere of drawing-room and concert-platform.
Weber, and Hummel himself, had written pieces
embodying the rhythms of Polish dances—
polonaises and so on—but none the less wholly
salon-pieces. The Rondeau à la mazurka is a salon-
piece too, but it is much nearer in spirit to the
simple peasant dance. (Almost as near as Schubert
in *his* dance music; indeed, despite Niecks's
remarks, a good deal of the piano-writing in this
piece is a good deal more like Schubert than true
Chopin.) The very first bar shows that we are not
to be fobbed off with superficial imitation of the
mere rhythms of the mazurka. The key is F major,
the third note a B natural.

Now the Lydian mode—the normal major scale
with the fourth degree sharpened—is very common
in Polish folk music.[1] Of the twelve examples of
Polish folk music quoted by Niecks (admittedly
'chosen with a view rather to illustrate Chopin's
indebtedness to Polish folk music than Polish folk
music itself'), six have the sharpened fourths. The
Mazurka in A minor, Op. 68, No. 2, written at
about the same time as the Rondeau à la mazurka,

[1] And also found in Russian folk music, perhaps as the result of
Polish influence. It is noteworthy, though perhaps only accidental,
that Mussorgsky introduces the sharpened fourth in the polonaise
of *Boris Godunov*.

also has the sharpened fourth, and we shall find it again and again in Chopin's later mazurkas. These harsh B naturals in the chief subject of the Rondeau are alone sufficient to sweep away any suggestion of that pleasant, superficially polished type of art suggested at the period by the name 'rondo'. (Even a rondo in 3/4 time, instead of 2/4, was something of a novelty.) But the implications of these B naturals go deeper than this: they show how thoroughly the young Chopin's musical mind must have been impregnated with the idiom of his native folk music if he could think in it as naturally and spontaneously as he does here. And there is the harmonic aspect too. After four bars of bare octaves Chopin begins to harmonize his melody. How then does he solve the problem of this awkward sharpened fourth? By harmonizing it with the very same characteristic chord that we have already noticed in the coda of the Variations sur un air national allemand: the second inversion of the diminished seventh on the sharpened fourth.[1] Is there not something more than coincidence in this hand-in-glove fitting of a favourite harmonic effect to a specifically Polish melodic effect? The chord itself was by no means new—Beethoven uses it in his very first piano sonata—but it is surely not too fanciful to suppose that Chopin's remarkable

---

[1] Henceforth I do not propose to speak of inversions of diminished sevenths, or even of other chords, unless there is a special reason for doing so. A diminished seventh remains the same no matter how it is inverted, and inversions seldom affect the tonal functions—which are what matter principally—of other chords.

affection for it was due in the first place to its aptness
to that modal peculiarity of Polish folk melody.

For the rest the harmony of the Rondeau is not
yet strikingly individual. Yet there are more portents: for instance, the little chain of dominant
sevenths in descending fifths, on G, on C and on F,
leading back into the B flat theme, in bars 19–21 of
the *tranquillamente e cantabile* section. As we shall
see, such chains of dominant sevenths, each resolving, not on the expected simple triad, but on the
expected triad *plus* an additional seventh, became
a common feature of Chopin's mature harmonic
style. Characteristic, too, is the *dolente* delay before
the actual return of the graceful B flat tune; both
the delay itself and the chord by which it is effected,
an inversion of the minor form of the added sixth,
are not only true romantic traits, but typically
Chopinesque.

There are similar slight but significant portents
in the actual piano-writing. Nothing yet very
individual, but a tendency to more widely spread
chords, a general—though only slight—loosening of
the texture as if the 'prentice composer were getting
more and more used to the feel of the sound-
material under his hands, able to work with it more
and more freely. But in this respect the Rondeau
à la mazurka is far surpassed by the 'Là ci darem'
Variations.

There is only the slightest element of virtuosity
in the Rondeau, but the Variations sparkle with
it from beginning to end. Let us be quite clear
in our minds about this 'virtuosity'. Even in this

avowed show-piece, Chopin's virtuosity is by no means that of the mere showman. His outward brilliance—and Liszt's, too, in a great many cases—is the natural manifestation of an inward exuberance, an exuberance generated by the consciousness of his own powers as a pianist. And if Liszt sometimes turns exuberantly to his audience, Chopin seems rather to be naïvely exulting in his command of the keyboard for his own private satisfaction. This inward spirit of virtuosity, this joy in freely and easily playing with one's sound-material and one's instrument, is manifest not only in the obvious bravura—the fioriture of the introduction, the triplet trills *staccato*, *ma leggiero e sempre più piano*, the tumultuous demisemiquaver rush of the second variation (anticipating the finale of the B flat minor Sonata), the bold, leaping *moto perpetuo* fourth, the dazzling finale—but in less spectacular traits: delicate washes of colour (bar 19 of the introduction and again the *delicato* passages just before the end of the introduction), the triplet counterpoint of the first variation, and above all the wide spread of the chords and of figures based on them.[1] In the introduction one finds chords spread over nearly two octaves in the left hand and, simultaneously, more than two in the right. From *Là ci darem* onwards, Chopin's figuration is no

[1] The second part of Variation 5, *cantabile e molto legato*, which so remarkably anticipates the love-scene in Strauss's *Heldenleben*, provides a curious instance of what one might call virtuosity of emotional expression. This is Don Giovanni, the supreme virtuoso in the technique of love-making.

longer octave-bound. That in itself necessitated a
far more advanced pedal technique than anyone had
employed hitherto. Chopin's own pedal markings
for these Variations, given in the Oxford Edition,
are of the greatest interest.

The variation form, of course, offered Chopin an
easy way of escape from a problem that he never
satisfactorily solved in these early days, and only
sometimes and with difficulty in later years,
except perhaps in a few works of his very latest
period, a problem that he usually contrived to
avoid: that of large-scale musical architecture. His
youthful fondness for rondo form is symptomatic,
for the rondo is potentially the loosest and most
rudimentary of the larger musical forms—and
Chopin makes the most of its possibilities. By
comparison with the mature Beethoven sonata-
rondo type, these early rondos of Chopin's, and
even the finali of the Concertos, seem hardly
musical organisms at all. They are essentially
nothing but stringings together of smaller independent entities, though in the case of Op. 5, the all-
pervading mazurka rhythm does give the piece a
pleasant semblance of unity. We shall find Chopin
later devoting special attention to the art of transition, which can skilfully conceal the joins of such
sectional compositions. But even in the Second
Impromptu, written ten years after the pieces we
are discussing now, we shall see him failing lamentably, and in these early rondos the seams show all
too plainly.

Of course, formal 'stringing together' instead of

organic form is inherent in the style of a composer
who thinks lyrically, as Chopin mainly did. It is an
extension on the grand scale of that process of
balancing melodic phrase by melodic phrase which,
with a lyrical composer, takes the place of the
motive-evolution of a Beethoven.   Admittedly,
Chopin, even in his early works (e.g. the three
Mazurkas, Op. 68, and the B flat subject of the
Rondeau à la mazurka) shows a paradoxical
predilection for melodic lines arising from the play
of tiny motives instead of developing in free
cantilena. But that, as Ernst Bücken was I think
the first to point out,[1] is also a pecularity of the
folk mazurka.[2] Chopin absorbed it into his musical
system in the composition of his own mazurkas,
and it quickly became one of the most striking traits
of his melodic style. (The Grande Valse brillante,
Op. 18, is an obvious example that one thinks of
immediately, but Chopin's music is full of far more
subtle and interesting cases of motive-generated
melody, e.g. the superb Étude in E Op. 10, No. 3,

---

[1] *Die Musik des 19. Jahrhunderts bis zur Moderne*. Potsdam. 1929.

[2] For instance, the tune, said to be 'popular in the neighbour-
hood of Warsaw', illustrating the article 'Mazurka' in *Grove*:

Ex. 6

and the third-period Nocturne, Op. 55, No. 2.)
All the same, a melody evolved from a single
motive is still a melody, not a theme; the music of
which it forms the backbone still remains lyrical so
long as the composer closes his ears to its latent
possibilities for development. And the young
Chopin did close his ears.

The first movement of the C minor Sonata
suggests that he may have convinced himself that
he was incapable of development on Beethovenian
lines; this very experiment proves that in these
early days he was. He worked here with true
themes, not with motive-inspired melodies, but
even allowing for the fact that the material is
incredibly dull and sterile—the whole Sonata is so
evidently a student-exercise that it is difficult to
understand why Chopin should have sent it to a
publisher[1]—his complete inability to develop
anything from it is really remarkable. Ernest
Newman's celebrated jeer at 'the average academy-
made composer with his tiresome and futile
attempts to make living music by the mechanical
manipulation of a couple of arid "subjects", remind-
ing us of nothing so much as some poor patient
Hottentot rubbing two dry sticks together in the
hope of getting a bit of fire', might well have been
suggested by Chopin's first movement, except that
Chopin rather suggests an insane Hottentot
rubbing a stick against nothing at all.

[1] Who, however, had the good sense to forget it for twenty-
three years, and published it only in July 1851, two years after the
composer's death.

The whole Sonata is lifeless, and—with the exception of a few bars in the second section of the trio that suggest the Chopin of the valses and mazurkas—completely un-Chopinesque. Even the piano-writing is extraordinarily dull and conservative; perhaps because the young composer felt that any suggestion of virtuosity was incompatible with pseudo-classical sonata-composition.

The whole work demonstrates both that the young Chopin's mind was incapable of generating living musical substance from a compact theme, and that he had no conception, other than the driest textbook conception, of the first principles of sonata-form. If any confirmation were needed—it is not—one would find it in the first movement of the G minor Trio, which we know was written in 1828; from the textbook point of view the student had made considerable progress—and he certainly wrote better music here—but he was just as far as ever from organic development and organic form.

The two other big show-pieces for piano and orchestra dating from this period, the Fantaisie sur des airs nationaux polonais, Op. 13, and the Krakowiak (Grand Rondeau de Concert, Op. 14) both dodge this problem of form in the ways indicated by their titles. The rondo was to the young Chopin an ever present help in time of structural trouble. As for the Fantaisie, it does not make even a decent pretence of being anything but a string of variations on one theme after another, each section being cobbled on to the next with hardly a semblance of art or artifice, and each being happily forgotten once it is done with. And yet these two show-pieces, written simply as vehicles for the composer's virtuosity, slight as their artistic value may be, are by no means without interest. They are deservedly forgotten by pianists but they must not be overlooked by the student of Chopin's slowly maturing style.

They are full of the lights and shadows of coming events. Not of actual passages of course, though, as Niecks points out, the first variation on the air 'Juz miesiac zaszedl' ('The moon had set') in the Fantaisie 'contains the germ of the charming Berceuse'; but full of anticipations of characteristic technical devices in the harmony and the *facture* for piano. The bravura writing is free and dashing but, except for the now almost invariable wide spread of the chords and figures, not remarkable. But the filigree ornamentation of the quieter passages already suggests the Chopin of the later nocturnes much more definitely than anything in the only slightly earlier Nocturne in E minor, Op. 72, No. 1.

The *largo* introduction to the Fantaisie particularly repays study from this point of view. The essence of Chopin's filigree style, as of Field's and Hummel's, is the throwing of a lacy and mainly chromatic veil by the right hand over a firm basis of diatonic broken chords in the left. Though Chopin's left-hand chords are more widely spread and hence more sonorous than Hummel's (but not more than Field's frequently are), so long as he is content to draw filmy single-note arabesques in the treble, *delicatissimo* and *leggierissimo*, as he does in this introduction, he is simply copying Field and Hummel. Even his irregular groupings of demi-semiquavers in thirteens and thirty-threes over steadily rocking quavers were no innovation. In the *Larghetto a capriccio* of his Sonata in D major, Op. 106, Hummel had spun chromatic fioriture in groups of 37, 34, 17, 19, and 15 demisemiquavers that are more Chopinesque than a good deal of early Chopin. (On the light Viennese pianos that Hummel played, such effects were easy and exquisite; Chopin, too, played on and wrote for pianos with a much lighter touch than ours—on which his silvery washes of delicate colour suffer transmutation, without the greatest care, into vulgar display passages.) But in the introduction to the Polish Fantasia Chopin no longer limits himself to simple fioriture. He had already hinted in the introduction to the 'Là ci darem' Variations (bar 19) that he knew other ways of chromatically embroidering a plain diatonic chord; now he freely employs double notes and introduces a new and altogether delicious appoggiatura technique:

Ex. 7

One passage near the beginning is specially prophetic of the mature Chopin:

Ex. 8

The emphasis obtained by the combination of the quintuplet and the novel flowering into significance of the inside part is as characteristic as the unexpected sharpening of the E and the consequent enharmonic twist on to the subdominant minor chord.

In both these examples the music is as fundamentally diatonic as anything in Hummel. But in one or two passages of the Fantaisie and Krakowiak —and at the peroration of the 'Là ci darem' Variations, sixteen bars before the end—Chopin breaks up the diatonic surface into a coruscating shower of chromatic particles:

Ex. 9

(a) Là ci darem

(b) **Polish Fantasia**
Brillante

(c) **Krakowiak**
Allegro non troppo

In each case the same thing has happened. To change the metaphor: Chopin has stepped from firm diatonic ground on to his favourite diminished seventh on the sharpened fourth, and taking off from that slippery point, danced giddily in the air through a sequence of diminished sevenths from the last of which he springs adroitly back to firm ground. In two of the three cases the chord is simply 'side-slipped' bodily, semitone by semitone; in Ex. 9b the effect is subtilized by repeating each chord in an inversion and then making the semitonal side-slip. In each case the effect is the same. It is notorious that any diminished seventh is tonally ambiguous; its key can be determined only from its context. And here we have a whole series of diminished sevenths of which only the first and last can be even fleetingly related to a key at all. In other words there has been a temporary sus-

pension of the principle of tonality. Atonality, at
any rate as a passing phenomenon, has become a
fact.

Indeed it had done so already long before
Chopin. As long ago as 1763 Haydn had ended
the exposition of a Symphony in E (No. 12 in the
Breitkopf *Gesamtausgabe*) with a firm dominant
unison B and opened the development with this
mysterious passage:

Ex. 10

Three years later we find Jommelli writing in his
Vologeso:

Ex. 11

and again in Gluck's *Iphigénie en Aulide* (Clytemnestra's 'Jupiter, lance ta foudre') (1774) and in Méhul's *Ariodant* (1799):

Ex. 12

The almost consonant sound of the chord made such successions easily acceptable to the ear, and even Chopin's admired Hummel, who was no harmonic revolutionist, has

Ex. 13

in his early Sonata in E flat, Op. 13.

But few things are more fatuous than a discussion of technical processes that leaves out of account the spirit in which the processes are applied. This particular device was not new in itself, but Chopin's use of it was quite unprecedented. Haydn had employed it as a 'surprise' effect; it must be one of the earliest of his numerous attempts to *épater les aristocrates*. Gluck and Jommelli and Méhul use it to emphasize points of dramatic intensity. With Hummel it is (shall we say?) purely musical, a touch of colour only in the sense that it does relieve the penny-plain E-flatness of its surroundings with a passing touch of twopenny chromaticism. Chopin, too, uses it in a purely musical sense. But how differently! In his pianist's hands it becomes a prism breaking up the white diatonic light into glittering rainbow particles. It has now become purely pianistic, reborn under a virtuoso's fingers and possible only in terms of piano timbre. And if still only a parenthetic effect, it is no longer so briefly transitory as in Hummel; in the Variations it lasts for four bars, though only two are quoted in Ex. 9*a*. The tiny crack in the firm tonal surface has widened perceptibly.

But filigree ornamentation and interesting little splashes of harmonic colour do not make master-pieces. The Fantaisie and the Krakowiak are simply bravura show-pieces, inferior in musical value even to the 'Là ci darem' Variations. If the introduction to the Fantaisie contains a number of the technical ingredients of the later nocturnes, it is almost completely devoid of their poetry. One must agree with Niecks that 'the best parts of the works, those that contain the greatest amount of music, are certainly the exceedingly spirited Kujawiak' (the last section of the Fantaisie) 'and the Krakowiak'. In other words, those based on folk material. For the Kujawiak is, on the admission of the title, an *air national polonais* and the principal theme of the Krakowiak is a variant of one quoted by Grove[1] as the tune to which the celebrated Fanny Elssler danced the *cracovienne* about 1840. 'Whether it is a real krakoviak, or a mere imitation, the writer is unable to say', he remarks. It is possibly a debasement, and Chopin's version a refinement, of a common original. On the other hand, both may be true folk variants of the kind familiar to students of the folk music of all countries.

The kujawiak is a species of mazurka—according to all the authorities the slowest kind of mazurka, though Chopin marks his *vivace*—and the non-bravura parts of this specimen are so like Chopin's early mazurkas that one sees immediately, even if one has not realized before, how close he remained in these works to authentic folk melody. And not to melody alone. The influence of the drone bass, also characteristic of the folk mazurka, is apparent, and the influence of the Lydian mode peeps out in the harmony (bar 7) long before it appears for a moment in the melody (bars 29 and 31). But before long the naïve peasant dance loses its character and becomes a brilliant concert-piece; the pianist has been too much for the Pole.

The mazurkas actually so-called written at this time, the three published posthumously as Op. 68, Nos. 1, 2, and 3, are completely devoid of any element of virtuosity. They are piano music only in the sense that Schubert's Ländler are piano music and might easily be simple transcriptions of

[1] *Dictionary of Music and Musicians* (3rd ed.) Article, 'Krakoviak'.

authentic peasant mazurkas. Between them they
represent the three main types of mazurka (all
characterized by the accent on the third beat[1]) :
the quick oberek or obertas (No. 1), the slow and
melancholy kujawiak (No. 2), strikingly unlike the
example so-called in the Fantaisie, and the intermediate type that has given its name to the whole
family, the mazur (No. 3). All three possess the
characteristics of the folk mazurka: love of the
sharpened fourth (opening of No. 2 and middle
section of No. 3), introduction of triplets in the
melody (No. 1), play with tiny motives (all three),
drone bass (whether stylized into an unobtrusive
pedal as in the opening of No. 2 or emphasized in
primitive open fifths as in the middle sections of the
same piece and of No. 3), the feminine ending of the
piece (even if only suggested by the left hand as in
No. 2), and of course the characteristic rhythms and
melodic patterns of the folk mazurkas throughout.

Nothing could be squarer than the construction,
entirely in four- or eight-bar periods. The harmony
is as impersonal as the piano-writing. Only a
tendency to thicken out melodies in sweet thirds
and sixths—also noticeable here and there in other
early works—must have come from the duets of
contemporary Italian opera rather than from the
music of the Polish peasants. Yet, with all this
squareness and a lack of finish amounting almost
to crudeness, despite the complete absence of

---

[1] According to some authorities, the mazur takes the accent on
the second beat.

Chopinesque piano-poetry, one feels that this is the real Chopin, working not only in a congenial medium but on a scale that in no way embarrasses him. These early mazurkas have none of the polish of the good miniature, yet form and content perfectly match—if only because the form simply arises (as it should) from the naïve, square-cut content.

The three polonaises, Op. 71, written at the same time as these mazurkas (1827–29) and, like them, published only posthumously, stand in the same relation to the later polonaises as their companions to the mature mazurkas. And the polonaises in general are more interesting in structure, harmony, and pianistic texture than the mazurkas. Whereas the mazurka is a naïve peasant dance, the polonaise was sophisticated, the dance of the Polish aristocracy—indeed less a dance than a processional ceremony—and this is reflected in Chopin's music. The polonaise offered no folk idiom to be absorbed, but all the same it observed certain well-marked conventions which Chopin adopted either simply or in stylized forms. Apart from the all-pervading accompaniment rhythm $\frac{3}{4}$ ♫ ♫♫ there were certain rhythmic formulae for the end of the melody: e.g. ♫♫ ♪ ♪, or ♫♫ ♫♫ and it is interesting to see how Chopin has refined and subtilized the latter figure in the final bars of all three of these polonaises. Another characteristic of the traditional polonaise is a tendency to repeat motives:

Ex. 14

a process not unrelated to the slightly different motive-play of the folk mazurka. This, too, is reflected in Chopin, and more clearly in these early polonaises (e.g. the opening of Op. 71, No. 2) than in the more mature ones. On the other hand, the influence of Weber's polonaises is not yet entirely thrown off, though it is much less obvious than in the G sharp minor Polonaise of 1822; even the figuration suggests a mingling of Weberian with purely Chopinesque traits.

One notes the shimmer of chromatically descending diminished sevenths again (near the end of the D minor) and the reappearance in a more subtle form (in Op. 71, No. 2) of the chain-of-dominant-sevenths device already noticed in the Rondeau à la mazurka[1] (bars 20–6 of the middle section). And the modulation made by taking the last dominant seventh of the chain as a German sixth in the new key became one of Chopin's favourite bits of sleight-of-hand. Eight bars after this last-mentioned passage (i.e. bars 18–19 before the *da capo*) occurs another typically Chopinesque harmonic effect: the dominant seventh changes from first inversion to root position by semitonal movement of the outside parts, thus producing transitional chords that have no tonal function.

[1] See p. 10.

Structurally these polonaises are very simple but less primitive than the mazurkas of the same period. While the latter are cast in the simplest ternary form, ABA, modified only by a slight curtailment of the repeat of the A section in Op. 68, Nos. 2 and 3, and keep within a very limited range of keys, the polonaises show that form carried to a higher power, as it were, each section being itself in ternary form. The range of keys in each piece is much wider and the second part of the central section of the B flat Polonaise—the crown of its structural arch and the part containing the interesting harmonic features just mentioned— is a sort of rudimentary development section. As in the mazurkas the dance-form 'excuses' the abruptness of the transitions, while the all-pervading dance rhythm unifies the whole.

Neither the three Valses (Op. 69, No. 2, Op. 70, No. 3, and the posthumous E minor) nor the single Nocturne (Op. 72, No. 1) of this period possess any interest beyond that attaching to early essays in forms in which Chopin was later to create masterpieces. Chopin's valses as a whole are much simpler harmonically than his other compositions. But even here an important part is played by harmonic effects for their own sake. Consider the second section of the E minor Valse; it begins with two apparently quite different eight-bar phrases which prove on examination to be both based on the same harmonic progression. The original conception must have been harmonic, the quasi-melodic figuration an afterthought. Both the motive-generated melodic pattern of the first phrase and the sequential treatment of the motive are characteristic of Chopin's melodic style. (Compare also bars 13–15 of the same Valse and the middle section of Op. 70, No. 3.)

Formally, too, these three Valses are extremely simple, though the E minor—in every way the most interesting—shows Chopin in more open revolt against the rule of symmetry in ternary form. In the Mazurka, Op. 68, No. 3, trusting to that principle of musical form which has been aptly compared with perspective foreshortening, he had cut down the repeat of the A section by half; sixteen bars heard now do quite satisfactorily balance thirty-two bars heard earlier, at a little distance in the memory. In the E minor Valse Chopin carries this principle still further by drastically reducing the repeat of A to a mere eight bars— extended, it is true, by a twenty-seven-bar coda arising out of them. The Nocturne in the same key is also extremely simple in build, though here it is the middle section that is disproportionately short[1] and the repeat is given mild additional interest by the not very characteristic ornamentation of the melody. The nine-bar phrase that concludes the first section at least shows that Chopin was aware of the booby-trap of square phrase-building in these small lyrical forms.

Otherwise, this first of all the nocturnes is curiously uncharacteristic. In style—*cantabile* right-hand melody over quiet, wide-spread triplet

---

[1] In some of the later Nocturnes (e.g. Op. 9, No. 1, and Op. 27, No. 1) the middle section is disproportionately long.

arpeggios—it is hardly distinguishable from a number of Field's nocturnes (e.g. Nos. 1, 2, and 5) and it lacks Field's peculiar idyllic charm. It appears to be a composition exercise. For the earliest specimens of the true romantic Chopin nocturne, we must turn to the slow movements of the two Concertos.

With the Concertos we at last reach the earliest of Chopin's works that have kept their places in the ordinary repertoire. Not very prominent places, perhaps; they are immature and even the warmest of Chopin's admirers must admit that they are poor examples of the piano concerto as such. But they—particularly their slow movements—contain far too much beautiful music to be allowed to follow the 'Là ci darem' Variations and the Fantasia on Polish Airs into the oblivion of dictionaries and history books.

It is useless to look in these two works for the beauties of concerto-form that one finds in Mozart and Beethoven. Like the Variations and Fantaisie and Krakowiak, they must be considered purely and simply ·as large-scale show-pieces for the soloist, with necessary but regrettable orchestral backgrounds. After the opening ritornello the orchestra's share is more or less limited to brief interjections and the provision of a light harmonic support to the solo. Niecks said of the orchestral accompaniments of the three earlier pieces that they show 'an inaptitude in writing for any other instrument than the piano that is quite surprising considering the great musical endowments of

Chopin in other respects'. And that is true also of the Concertos—where the inevitable long tuttis show up the inadequacy of the orchestration far more pitilessly than any of the short passages in the earlier works—and of the Grande Polonaise brillante for piano and orchestra written at about the same time. It is significant that after this Chopin never wrote for orchestra again.[1]

The perfunctory treatment of the orchestra in the Concertos, however, must be attributed not only to Chopin's unhappiness in handling it, but to the example of his model, Hummel. Hummel also had given the orchestra a merely subordinate role in his concertos and his lead was followed not only by Chopin, but by most of the second- and third-rate concerto composers of the romantic dawn: Field, Kalkbrenner, Moscheles, and the rest. Fundamentally, this school derived from Johann Christian Bach. In the hands of the great Bach's sons, the genre Klavierkonzert[2] had split into two main types. C. P. E. Bach, who kept faithfully to

---

[1] One peculiarity of Chopin's scoring is worth notice: the puzzling inclusion in both concertos of a part for a single trombone. It can hardly be a mere coincidence that Glinka's Night in Madrid and Kamarinskaya, also written specially for a Warsaw orchestra, though nearly twenty years later, likewise contain parts for a single bass trombone. Obviously Warsaw possessed only one respectable trombonist. But he must have been a good player; Glinka tells us in his memoirs that the Governor's Kapellmeister, Pohlenz, 'orchestrated my Prayer' (a piano piece) 'with trombone obbligato and it was not ineffective'.

[2] Which had come into existence in Johann Sebastian's generation as an offspring of the violin concerto.

the true concerto idea, the interplay of solo and tutti each equally important, stands at the head of the great line of heredity that runs through the later Mozart and Beethoven to Brahms. On the other hand, Johann Christian Bach, who sacrificed the dialogue principle to the importance of the solo instrument, which he provided with brilliant passage-work as well as a half-Italian cantabile type of melody (and who incidentally introduced the rondo finale), became the forefather of the virtuoso concerto of the younger Mozart, Hummel, Field, and Chopin. And of this type in the early nineteenth century Hummel was indisputably the most skilful practitioner.

Arnold Schering[1] suggests a non-Hummelian model for Chopin's E minor Concerto: the Grand Concerto in D minor, Op. 61, of Kalkbrenner to whom the Chopin work is actually dedicated. He draws attention to 'a certain relationship between Kalkbrenner's opening:

Ex. 15

and Chopin's, particularly noticeable in the bass', and goes on to point out other features common to both—but, unfortunately for his theory, also to a good many other concertos of the same period. If Schering had not been led astray by the dedication of the E minor Concerto, he might have

[1] *Geschichte des Instrumentalkonzerts.* Second Edition. Leipzig, 1927.

noticed that the opening of the earlier F minor work,[1] with its minor thirds descending chromatically, is really more akin to the Kalkbrenner. And if he had looked a little more closely at the opening of Hummel's Concerto in A minor, Op. 85, he would have found an actual identity of certain motives in it and in the opening of the Chopin E minor:

Ex. 16

(a) Hummel
Allegro moderato

(b) Chopin
Allegro maestoso risoluto

In this light Chopin's theme is seen to be essentially an elaboration and extension of the older master's and at the same time a considerable improvement on it, longer-breathed, rising and falling in one big eight-bar curve. Notwithstanding which, Chopin was completely unable to evolve from it a living musical tissue.

Chopin's technical kinship with Hummel[2] and

---

[1] The later opus-number of the F minor and its general superiority are misleading. Op. 21 was composed in 1829; Op. 11 in 1830.

[2] He even writes for strings *col legno* in the finale of the F minor as Hummel had done.

his immense superiority are even more clearly demonstrated by comparison of the *larghetti* of both concertos with the corresponding movement of Hummel's B minor Concerto. Technically all three can be described in the same general terms: a brief orchestral preamble serves to introduce a prolonged solo of the nocturne-type, based on a simple melody (quickly flowering into delicious fioriture) played by the right hand in single notes or octaves over a rocking quaver accompaniment in the left.[1] But Hummel's music is prose, Chopin's is poetry—sentimental, if you like, and inferior to his later poetry, but undeniably poetry. Hummel's is classical, or rather an imitation of the smooth outward form of classicism, Chopin's is romantic. Or in the more precise terms of style: Hummel's melody is square-cut and centres feebly on the

---

[1] Structurally both the Chopin slow movements are timid extensions of the ABA formula:

F minor:

Brief orchestral prelude.

A—Main theme (solo) in A flat.

A—The same repeated with further decorative elaboration (solo) (A flat).

B—Recitative for piano in octaves (A flat minor).

A—Main theme with fresh ornamentation (solo) (A flat). Brief orchestral postlude (on same material as prelude).

E minor:

Brief orchestral prelude.

A—Main theme (solo) in E major.

B—Secondary theme in B major (solo).

A—Main theme ornamented in E major (solo) and modulating through brief interludes in G sharp minor to—

B—Secondary theme in G sharp major (solo).

A—Main theme in orchestra, accompanied by piano figuration (E major).

notes of the common chord,[1] Chopin's—at least
in the F minor—pours out in a long-breathed,
sensitive, passionate cantilena proceeding mainly
in conjunct motion like a vocal melody and ornamented by exquisite piano-coloratura. We are face
to face, for the first time, with the miracle of
Chopin's nocturne-type of melody which *is* vocal in
essence, originating in a very different type of
music from Hummel's: Italian opera in general and
Bellini's in particular. Chopin's general indebtedness to Bellini will be discussed later but it is worth
pointing out here in passing that the operatic
flavour of the F minor slow movement is heightened
by its recitative-like middle section, the accompaniment to which (tremolo string chords with
ominous double-bass pizzicati) is, as Tovey says,[2]
'as fine a piece of instrumention as Berlioz could
have chosen to quote in his famous treatise'.

The final movements of both concertos are likewise Hummelian rondos: the F minor by Hummel
out of the mazurka, the E minor even more Hummelian and rather superficial in its charm, though
with one touch of humour almost worthy of Beethoven—the reappearance of the principal theme a
semitone flat, a 'mistake' which is not corrected till
eight bars later. Chopin repeated the jest some
years later in the F sharp Impromptu.

But in the concerto, as in the symphony, it is the
first movement by which a work stands or falls.
And in the structure of their first movements the

---

[1] As does that of the *larghetto* of his A minor Concerto.
[2] *Essays in Musical Analysis.* Vol. iii. O.U.P. 1936.

two Chopin concertos, which neither stand nor fall but stumble, do not follow Hummel as slavishly as seems to be generally supposed. In both his A minor and his B minor Concertos Hummel works to precisely the same pattern, a pattern extraordinarily like that of Beethoven's much greater C minor. In that fictitious abstraction which the authors of textbooks on musical form call 'classical concerto form', the opening tutti presents both subjects[1] in the tonic key (as indeed is usually the case in Mozart), leaving them to be sorted out and tonally distributed by the soloist; Beethoven in the C minor and Hummel in both these concertos put their second subjects at once in the relative major in the first tutti. They agree also in winding up the first tutti with an extensive return to first-subject material in the tonic. Chopin follows them in the F minor in at once stating his second subject in the relative major, but not in returning to the first-subject material. In the E minor he makes the return to first-subject material but puts the second subject in the *tonic* major. In both he finally recapitulates the second subject in the relative major: in other words, in the F minor the reprise tamely follows the same unenterprising key-sequence as the exposition—the flouting of a basic principle of sonata-form—while in the E minor the same principle is turned completely on its head, the twofold exposition clinging stoutly to the tonic throughout, with a perverse shifting of tonic in the

---

[1] By 'subjects', of course, I mean not 'themes', but whole sections of music, each of which may contain several themes.

recapitulation. And whereas a greater master of
form might have contrived to commit all these
crimes and disguise them as strokes of genius.
Chopin merely demonstrates that the beauties of
key-relationship and key-balance perceived by all
the Viennese classical masters meant nothing to
him. Let us be thankful for that; if they had meant
a great deal to him, he might have given us two
rather better concertos but he would have found it
immensely more difficult later to break up that solid
diatonic system into the fascinating, constantly
modulating, frequently chromatic sound-texture
which constitutes about three-quarters of the real
Chopin and which opened the way for Liszt, Wagner, Debussy, and Schönberg.

Chopin's weakness of key-sense was equalled
only by the weakness of his sense of development,
the other main feature of the great classical concertos. The nearer he approaches to a passable
imitation of true development, the drier and less
Chopinesque the music becomes. Instead of growing up from the themes, it dwindles down from
them. Nothing flowers from them, even from the
promising opening of the E minor; Chopin can
only strive desperately to squeeze something out
of them. In the so-called development sections,
falling back on Hummelian precedent, he abandons
even the pretence of working out; the music consists simply of brilliant passage-work for the soloist
against which, in the F minor, the orchestra bandies
about fragments of the first-subject material mainly
on solo wind. In the E minor thematic relevance

is limited to the employment for about a dozen bars of the opening of Ex. 16*b* as a bass. As Niecks puts it, 'the pianoforte part reminds one too much of a study, without having the beauty of Chopin's compositions thus entitled'. The concertos as a whole, however, do show Chopin's keyboard writing—his filigree fioriture and his characteristic widespread passage-work—at the highest point it had reached so far. Technically they form together a complete encyclopaedia of the new keyboard idiom and a rich foretaste of the new harmonic idiom that developed in its train: dizzy chromatic side-slippings of dissonances, analogous to Ex. 9, the hard glitter of seventh-producing appoggiaturas, as at the end of the first movement of the E minor, and so on. But all this can be studied much more conveniently and to more purpose in the set of twelve Études, Op. 10, which are in so many respects quite mature and so fine that it seems a little unfair to class them with the works of Chopin's nonage merely on chronological grounds.

The Op. 10 Études enable one to see at a glance how far Chopin's technique had advanced beyond his predecessors by comparing each study with a slightly older one dealing with the same technical difficulty.[1] The very first in C major, for instance,

---

[1] The dedication, 'à son ami, F. Liszt', is not a tacit admission of indebtedness, by the way. Liszt's earliest studies, other than the boyish *Études pour le piano en douze Exercices* of 1826, did not appear till five or six years after Chopin's Op. 10, later even than his Op. 25.

with its tremendous striding arpeggios, covers the same technical ground as Cramer's Study in D minor (No. 19 in von Bülow's edition) but where Cramer's groups lie within fifths and sixths, Chopin's fill octaves; where Cramer asks for an octave stretch, Chopin demands a tenth. Similarly the left-hand accompaniment arpeggio in No. 9 covers elevenths and thirteenths as compared with Cramer's tenths and sixths in the parallel figure of his D major Étude (No. 53). And Chopin's No. 7 and No. 10, both very characteristic of his piano-style, similarly complicate the problems of Cramer's No. 52:

Ex. 17

and Clementi's Étude No. 23 (Tausig's edition):

Ex. 18

Again, more than one critic has drawn attention to the affinity between No. 2 in A minor and Moscheles' Étude in G, Op. 70, No. 3, likewise chromatic but artistically very inferior. But Chopin ties up the thumb and first finger of the right hand with inner harmonies, so that the rapid chromatic scales must be played with three fingers only: a reversion, as Leichtentritt points out, to a type of fingering used in the pre-Bach period. The enormous importance Chopin attached to this Étude is shown by the fingering, which he has given for every note except in repeated passages; no other composition in the whole of his music is so completely fingered; none demonstrates more clearly the importance of following the composer's own fingering and not that of his ingenious editors. The basic principle will be found to be the almost invariable use of the third finger (Continental style) for all black keys.

But the tackling of such awkward figures as those in Ex. 31, from the F major Étude, No. 8, and the tremendous spread chords in both hands of No. 11, were as completely new technically as were the profound tragic power of No. 12 and the sheer melodic loveliness of No. 3[1] musically.

The technical purpose of an étude can best be achieved by embodying the particular problem in a single motive or pattern which is persistently worked out all through the piece. And this basing of the whole composition on one motive, which has always been a peculiarity of the étude, solved for Chopin the real problem of miniature form: contrast and variety within a small unity. Even the purely melodic studies, Nos. 3 and 6, are based mainly on motive-generated melodies with regular-

[1] Speaking of No. 3 in E major, Niecks tells us that 'Chopin said to Gutmann that he had never in his life written another such beautiful melody'. Rimsky-Korsakov considered it the most perfect melody in all music, 'the very music of the Kingdom of Heaven'.

patterned accompaniments, and the all-pervading figure unifies each piece as do the dance-rhythms of the polonaise or mazurka, and does it much more organically. (Exactly as such Schubert songs as 'Auf dem Wasser zu singen' and 'Gretchen am Spinnrad' are held together by the accompaniment figure.) And whereas the clear-cut phrases of the dance and the alternations of its contrasting melodic ideas draw attention to joins and to the inevitable squareness of structure, the plastic nature of the single motive and the *moto perpetuo* character of most of the patterns in an étude conceal the joins and enormously simplify that business of transition which is one of the subtlest problems of the art of musical composition.

The broad outlines of these Etudes are simple enough. Like their successors in Op. 25, they are almost all cast in the simple, slightly modified ABA form, with or without coda, of the valses and mazurkas. But the middle section is usually marked not by new material but by contrast of key, colourful modulation, and varied treatment of the initial motive and technical problem; in fact, is not so much a trio as a miniature development section. There can be no development in the true sense, for there is usually no 'theme' to develop. But there is plenty of scope for that unconstrained, more or less improvisatory play with pianistic figures and colourful harmonic progressions in which Chopin delighted.

The great C minor, the so-called 'Revolution' Study, represents Chopin's supreme formal achievement up to the date (September, 1831) at which it was written. At least half a dozen different left-hand figures are employed, but they are all marked by regular semiquaver movement and this, together with the tragic declamatory right-hand melody, holds the whole together. The piece sounds as if dashed off in one great outburst of passionate feeling. The modulating middle section is swept in so naturally and leads so naturally back into the repeat, now wonderfully intensified; the repeat of the first section grows so naturally into the overpoweringly effective coda, the melody being simply augmented in double note-values; and this coda is so superbly conceived: that the simple underlying ternary form is quite unnoticed. Yet the piece is actually almost as squarely built as any of the early mazurkas:

A—8 bars introduction.
    Phrase of 2 + 8 bars.
    The same repeated, with the last 4 bars modified (say, 2 + 4 + 4) leading into—
B—Three 4-bar units, the last leading back into—
A—8 bars introduction.
    Phrase of 2 + 8 bars.
    Phrase of 2 + 4 + 4 bars, the last four being again different.
Coda—8 bars (growing out of the previous four by augmentation of the motive).
    4 bars based on the introduction figure, *sotto voce*.

4 bars based on the introduction figure,
ff ed appassionato.

The form is as simple as ever but it is now employed by a master instead of by a novice.

Harmonically, too, several of the Op. 10 Études announce Chopin's arrival at full mastery, so, instead of examining them separately from this point of view, I propose to group them with the other works of maturity in a general discussion of Chopin's harmonic style (pp. 77–95).

CHOPIN'S MATURE STYLE

(1831–1840)

THE compositions of Chopin's second period, those written after his arrival in Paris in 1831 and before the last change in style perceptible from about 1841 onwards, are as follows:

Ballades in G minor, Op. 23 (1831–5), and F, Op. 38 (1836–39)

Bolero, Op. 19 (1833)

Études, Op. 25, and Trois Nouvelles Études (1832–39)

Fantaisie-Impromptu, Op. 66 (1834)

Impromptus in A flat, Op. 29 (1837), and F sharp, Op. 36 (1839)

Mazurkas, Op. 17 (1832–3), Op. 24 (1834–5), Op. 67, Nos. 1 and 3 (1835), Opp. 30 and 33 (1836–38), Op. 41, (1838–9), in A minor (*Notre temps*) (1840).

Nocturnes, Op. 15, No. 3 (1833), Op. 27 (1834–5), Op. 32 (1836–7), Op. 37 (1838–9)

Polonaises, Op. 26 (1834–5) and Op. 40 (1838–9)

Preludes, Op. 28 (1836–39)

Rondo in E flat, Op. 16 (1832)

Scherzos in B minor, Op. 20 (1831–2), B flat minor, Op. 31 (1837), and C sharp minor, Op. 39 (1839)

Sonata in B flat minor, Op. 35 (1839)

Valses, Op. 18 (1831), Op. 69, No. 1 and
Op. 70, No. 1 (1835), Op. 34 (1831–38), Op. 42
(1840)

Variations brillantes (on an air from Hérold's
Ludovic), Op. 12 (1833)

Some of these are of little importance. The
Bolero, the E flat Rondo, and the Op. 12 Variations can be entirely left out of account, though
even the least characteristic work of the three, the
Variations, contains a passage, the *lento* variation
in D flat, that could hardly have been written by
anyone else. It is bad Chopin; just how bad may
be seen very easily by comparing it with the D
flat Nocturne, Op. 27, No. 2; but unmistakable
Chopin for all that. The remaining compositions
of this period include much of his finest and most
characteristic work. It is no longer necessary to
trace his artistic development step by step. We
can stand back a little and look at this output as a
whole from various points of view: form, melody,
harmony, and keyboard style in general.

Chopin's form is generally considered to be his
weakest point. It was also the weakest point of all
his contemporaries. And, of course, compared
with Beethoven's—a fantastically unfair comparison—his sense of form is primitive, being
limited almost exclusively to the possibilities of
more or less modified ternary form. The elemen-
tary formula ABA is the structural basis of the vast
majority of Chopin's shorter pieces. It underlies
the majority of his second-period mazurkas, all

his second-period polonaises,[1] and practically all the second-period nocturnes. Its predominance in the études has already been mentioned—Nos. 1 and 3 of the Trois Nouvelles Études are the only exceptions—and it is either implicit or explicit in a number of the preludes. Only the valses tend to break away into looser patterns akin to the 'suite of waltzes' initiated by Hummel in 1808 (*Tänze f.d. Apollo Saale*, Op. 31) and familiar through the works of the Strausses, Lanner, and Gung'l. Ternary form is, as we shall see presently, even the basis of the larger forms evolved by Chopin: the scherzo, the impromptu, and the ballade.

But, admitting the primitive nature of Chopin's basic conception of form, one can have nothing but praise for the skill with which he so often modifies, adapts, or even completely conceals this naïve basis. We have already seen something of this in the great C minor Étude, Op. 10, No. 12. And we have already noticed in the Mazurka, Op. 68, No.

[1] The vital *da capo* mark at the end of the second part of the C sharp minor Polonaise, Op. 26, No. 1, is missing in some editions. This has misled Leichtentritt (*Analyse der Chopin'sche Klavierwerke*) into condemnation of the 'not quite satisfactory binary form'. Leichtentritt's book, not to be confused with his earlier biographical *Friedrich Chopin*, contains far too many slips of this kind. Although the most detailed analysis of Chopin's works so far published, and a book which I myself have found very useful, its value is seriously diminished by innumerable errors in both text and music-type, I have found Leichtentritt's views on Chopin's harmony—views sometimes self-contradictory—of hardly any use at all.

3, and the posthumously published Valse in E
minor the 'perspective foreshortening' of the
return to the first section. This curtailing of the
third section of the ABA form became the rule
rather than the exception with Chopin, and it is
interesting to note how the same proportion of
third section is retained even in some of the most
drastically curtailed instances; for instance, in the
Prelude in B minor, Op. 28, No. 6, this third
section consists of four out of the twenty-six bars
of the whole piece, in the Mazurka in the same key,
Op. 33, No. 4, of thirty-two bars out of two hundred and twenty-odd, in the C sharp minor Nocturne, Op. 27, No. 1, of eighteen bars out of just
over a hundred: that is, in each case, of about a
sixth of the whole piece. The same proportion is
felt again in the C minor Polonaise, Op. 40, No. 2,
which is in a sort of compound ternary form with
the last two sections amputated: ABA CDC A.

Chopin often offers some sort of compensation
for this curtailment; he does not trust solely to one's
sense of perspective to restore the balance. In the
Polonaise just mentioned he takes a little three-
note motive, E flat, C, B flat (which may or may
not have been derived from the principal theme of the
piece, but which at any rate was utterly insignificant when it appeared before in a parallel passage),
builds it up for four bars to a climactic point
marked by the actual return of the first theme, and
then accompanies that theme with a motive derived
from the E flat-C-B flat idea. The object is not merely
to conceal the join, which is done quite skilfully, but

to give additional weight and breadth to an archi-
tectural section that has been robbed of a good deal
of length.

In other cases, for instance the C sharp minor
Nocturne and the D flat Prelude, the compensation
takes the form of a new idea introduced in the coda:
in the former, one of astonishing freshness and
beauty. Chopin's codas are often memorable as
perfect roundings-off of perfect poems, but, as
here, they not infrequently have a structural function as well. (On the other hand, his introductions
are seldom important structurally; they serve only to
attract attention, or in his later works, more subtly,
to place a harmonic curtain before the tonic key
and so heighten the effect of its first appearance.)[1]
In one piece, the B major Nocturne, Op. 32, No. 1,
the extremely dramatic coda entirely takes the
place of a repeat of the first section. At the end of
the middle portion, which is actually related to the
first by its stretto cadences, the music glides down
to a dominant seventh which is succeeded, not by
the expected tonic chord and opening theme, but
by a foreign chord, drumlike throbs, and a tragic
recitative: perhaps the most Wagnerian of all the
numerous passages in which Chopin anticipates
Wagner.

In the B flat Prelude, Op. 28, No. 21, the repeat

[1] See, tor instance, the Mazurka, Op. 30, No. 4, the Scherzo in
C sharp minor, and the Sonata in B flat minor, all written on
the very eve of the third period. There were plenty of classical
precedents for the use of this tonal curtain, but the Viennese
masters rarely employed it with Chopin's subtlety.

is not drastically replaced by an entirely new
element as in this nocturne; but only the chromatic
accompaniment figure returns, now in its own independent right, rises to a climax (the peak of the
whole prelude), dies down in a passage exactly
parallel to one in the early part, but now entirely
changed in significance, and spontaneously gen-
erates a new coda figure. The piece is one of the
finest examples of Chopin's formal art on the tiny
scale, for the rudimentary ternary form is completely transfigured.

Nor was his skill limited to this very miniature
type of piece. Of all Chopin's smaller compositions
the most sectionalized, next to the valses, are the
mazurkas. Sharply contrasting sections are natural
in dance-music and therefore perfectly justifiable
in glorified dance-music such as these, and even
when the composer relies on nothing more than
the all-pervading mazurka characteristics to hold
the piece together one is quite satisfied. But as
early as Op. 24, No. 4, he begins to be no longer
content with this. The piece is 'framed' by a
twelve-bar introduction and thirty-two-bar coda;
the main part of the mazurka grows out of the
introduction so spontaneously that one hardly
realizes that the opening, after the first four bars, is
still only introduction, especially as the main theme
of the mazurka is foreshadowed in bars 5 and 6;
the return of the first section is contrived under the
cloak of the capricious double-dotted figure which
first appears four bars after the first double-bar;
and the coda is based on the alto part of the

introduction (bars 6-8). Again in Op. 30, No. 4,
one of the first of those great mazurkas which are
much less dances than tragic poems, we find a coda
that not only looks back to the thematic introduction but combines

Ex. 19

the themes of both main and middle sections:

Ex. 20

With Op. 41, No. 1, an eve-of-third-period work,
we already reach the almost symphonic style of the
greatest mazurkas of the last phase. The return to
the first section and the transition to the coda are
both effected by quasi-development passages, so
that the general outline appears as:

A *a*—16 bars.
   b—16 bars.
B *c*—16 bars.
   d—16 bars.
      8 transition bars based on *a*.

A *a*—16 bars.
   b—16 bars.
        14 bars free continuation of *b*, building
        up to the—
Coda—8 bars of *a*.
        13 bars based on the inversion of a
        motive common to *b* and *d*.

Even in more simply constructed mazurkas similar
traits appear. Thus in Op. 41, No. 4, the greater
part of the middle section consists of a miniature
development of the opening theme.

Naturally, the more highly organized forms are
in the minority, yet many of even the simplest of
Chopin's maturer mazurkas and other short pieces
are given some little touch that lightly disguises the
naïveté of the underlying symmetry; the sections
are repeated, as in Op. 24, No. 3, and the Nocturne
Op. 27, No. 2, or the repeat takes a wrong turning
and ends deliciously and unexpectedly, as in Op.
30, No. 1. The A flat Valse, Op. 34, No. 1, disguises its ternary form by a 32-bar 'refrain' common
to each section—AX BX AX Coda—and the
straggling shape of Op. 42, in the same key, is held
together by the same simple device: AX BX CX
DX AX CX.

But, except in the suite-like valses, Chopin's
forms can seldom be accused of straggling. On the
few occasions when he does break away from the
fundamental ternary pattern it is nearly always
into the nearly related ABACA form: the primitive
rondo or scherzo-with-second-trio *à la Schumann*

(cf. the Mazurkas, Op. 6, No. 1, Op. 7, Nos. 1 and 4; Op. 24, No. 2; the Prelude, Op. 28, No. 17, etc.). There are exceptions—the varied strophes of the E flat Nocturne, Op. 9, No. 2, the perfect 'arch' (ABCBA) of the Mazurka in E minor, Op. 41, No. 2, the strange, but emotionally inevitable, 'continuous' form of the G minor Nocturne, Op. 15, No. 3—but they are remarkably rare.

One other factor must be taken into account in considering even the smallest forms in Chopin: that of variable interpretation. A section may be repeated note for note as far as the printed music is concerned, yet, if Chopin's own practice counts for anything, the repetition was not necessarily intended to be exact in performance. With some composers—for instance, Beethoven—the printed notes are an attempt to represent music ideally conceived by the brain and inward ear; that ideal must have been practically immutable and it is the interpreter's duty to seek it through the printed notes. Chopin's contact with his sound-medium was more immediate; the printed forms of his works were often, as his own numerous variants and changes of mind show, the records of music that, however finely polished and worked out, was originally and essentially keyboard improvisation; the record remained but the improviser's own moods constantly changed. If Chopin did not go so far as Liszt, who actually improvised virtuosic trimmings to his interpretations, the spirit of improvisation was always present in his playing. A. J. Hipkins, the pioneer of Chopin-playing in

England, who heard the composer at Broadwood's in 1848, says: 'Chopin *never* played his own compositions twice alike, but varied each according to the mood of the moment, a mood that charmed by its very waywardness.'[1] We may safely assume that what was true of his interpretation of whole compositions was also true in a modified degree of his reading of repeated sections of a work. And this view is sometimes confirmed by the composer's markings. The first eight bars of the Étude, Op. 10, No. 9, for instance, have no fewer than five minor *crescendo* markings and the third bar is marked *con forza*; the note-for-note repeat which follows is marked at the beginning *sotto voce* and has only one *crescendo* marking. It is obvious that Chopin wished the second eight bars to sound like an echo of the first eight rather than like a mere repetition of them. And if this principle of variable interpretation plays a part in even the small forms, it must be far more important in some of the large-scale works, the scherzi and impromptus, which are after all essentially only small forms magnified and in which there are long stretches of note-for-note repetition.

Of these large-scale works two of the ballades, three of the scherzi and two of the impromptus (plus the Fantaisie-Impromptu) belong to Chopin's second period. The impromptus represent the lowest type of organism, the scherzi a slightly higher type, the ballades an altogether new and largely successful hybrid form, half lyrical and

[1] *How Chopin Played.* Dent. 1937.

akin to the short pieces, half epic and related to the principle of sonata form. And then of course there is also the B flat minor Sonata itself.

The Impromptu in A flat, the Fantaisie-Impromptu, and the B minor Scherzo are structurally of little interest. They are merely large-scale ternary structures with the joins in the carpentry ill-concealed. Even the effective return of the main section of the B minor Scherzo—the *fortissimo* opening chords breaking in among the dying echoes of the Polish Christmas song 'Lulajže Jezuniu' ('Sleep, baby Jesus'), which is the basis of the middle section—is very naïve by comparison with the best of Chopin's later transitions. The beautiful Impromptu in F sharp is also essentially in ternary form, though nine-tenths of the interest of the piece lies in the enormously extended and elaborated return of the first section: first in the 'wrong' key, a semitone too low, as in the finale of the E minor Concerto, then in the right one, but more and more completely veiled by variation.[1] In this piece, too, occurs a weak transition, perhaps the clumsiest in the whole of Chopin, despite the comparatively late date of the composition (1838)

[1] The beautiful opening melodic phrase, which Brahms must have unconsciously recollected a quarter of a century later when he set Ludwig Hölty's 'Die Mainacht', is itself a slight variant of a Ukrainian folk tune used by Rimsky-Korsakov in his opera *May Night*. In view of the close connexion between Polish and Ukrainian folk music, it seems probable that Chopin took his theme directly from a Polish melody. The point of similarity between Brahms's and Rimsky-Korsakov's 'May Nights' is a curious coincidence but nothing more.

and the attempt to make the link organic or at least thematic; the modulation from the D major 'middle' section (which is by no means at the structural centre of gravity) to the F major return of the first theme consists of two bars which, as Huneker says,[1] 'creak on their hinges'. They creak partly because Chopin, dropping into a harmonic habit which had by that time become almost second nature to him, reduced the progression to a mere skeleton, comprehensible enough to him because he mentally clothed it with flesh:

Ex. 21

but sounding very queer to ears that hear only the actual sounds; partly because even when thus flayed alive and unrecognizable, this particular chord-progression still does not fit the fragment of theme at all comfortably. The ingenious return to F sharp, twelve bars later, is as effective as this is the reverse.

Even the most enthusiastic admirers of Chopin would hardly claim that the F sharp Impromptu is a masterpiece of form. Or the G minor Ballade either. Yet the Ballade is recognizably a first and not unsuccessful experiment in a new and entirely

---

[1] *Chopin: The Man and his Music.* William Reeves. 1901.

individual form, a form that politely touches its hat to the superficial features of the classical 'first movement' but quietly ignores most of its underlying principles. The 'arch'-like outline of the G minor is simple enough:

Introduction: *Largo*.

First subject (*moderato*): G minor.

Second subject (*meno mosso*): E flat.

Development (*a tempo*): beginning in A minor and passing through various keys.

Second subject: E flat.

First subject (drastically shortened): G minor.

Coda (*presto con fuoco*): G minor.

The irregular recapitulation, with the second-subject themes returning before the first subject and still in the contrasting key, had a precedent in the first movement of another famous romantic work also composed in Paris and only five or six years earlier: Berlioz's *Symphonie fantastique*. Chopin notoriously disliked Berlioz's music, but it seems probable that he had no objection to taking a hint from it. His 'development section' in the G minor Ballade is even less Beethovenian than Berlioz's; it consists rather of variation and improvisation than of true development. That was inevitable with such lyrical themes. But it fulfils the same structural function, with its perambulation through strange keys—though even here Chopin blunders upon E flat long before he is ready to get back to the business of recapitulation.

And there are other signs that Chopin was beginning to understand something of the real essence of sonata-form. For instance, that recapitulation is not merely repetition, that if things have really happened in the development one cannot, without artistic falsehood, tamely return to the *status quo ante*. Consider the treatment of the *meno mosso* second subject here. The apparently insignificant florid link in the exposition (bar 8) has grown in the development and thrown its tendrils over four bars of the theme; and in the recapitulation it is the quintuplet-crotchet idea evolved from this which dominates the whole passage.

The Second Ballade, Op. 38, is a modification of the same form, and there is good reason to suppose that its original version may have been constructed on exactly the same lines. Schumann, to whom it is dedicated, wrote that 'its impassioned episodes seem to have been afterwards inserted. I recollect very well when Chopin played the Ballade here; it finished in F major, now it closes in A minor'. What Schumann meant by 'its impassioned episodes' is not altogether clear; perhaps the powerful sequential passage that crowns the *presto con fuoco* second subject, perhaps the more strenuous incidents in the working out of the first subject, which follows this, or perhaps the stormy coda. But the return of the first subject is foreshadowed in the bass octave passage just before the coda and does actually occur, with dramatic effect, as a fleeting wistful reminiscence when this coda has reached its climax. Imagine, then, that, instead of the coda, heralded and rounded off by fragments of the first subject, Chopin had here simply written out the first subject in full and in F major; we should have a form almost exactly like that of the G minor Ballade. And it seems to me highly probable that this or something like it *was* the original form of the piece that Schumann heard.

But if Chopin did originally end the piece in this way, he must have felt the artistic falsity of such a conclusion. (Apart altogether from the fact that the Ballade was admittedly 'inspired by some poems of Mickiewicz' which presumably demanded a tragic ending.[1]) Accordingly he altered it, even its key, and the result is effective and highly dramatic. But in contriving a dramatically satisfactory form he was unable to avoid battering the purely musical form rather badly and the marks of his tinkering remain visible.

From the structural point of view, the scherzi are much less interesting than the ballades, but

[1] As far as I can discover, Chopin himself never admitted anything more definite than this. But Huneker, in *Chopin: the Man and his Music*, first commends him as a 'wise artist' for giving no more definite clue, and then goes on, without quoting any authority, to speak of 'the G minor Ballade, after *Konrad Wallenrod*', to assert that the Second Ballade was 'written, Chopin admits, under the direct inspiration of Adam Mickiewicz's *Le Lac de Willis*', and to speak of the A flat Ballade as 'the *Undine* of Mickiewicz'. (On the F minor he says nothing, though there is a sort of legend connecting it with the poem *Trzech Budrysów*.) Now Huneker was cursed not only with an unduly florid prose style but with a tendency to intellectual pretentiousness that only too often arouses suspicion that he was something of a charlatan. If he had ever read *Konrad Wallenrod*, he would have known that

even in these the idea of sonata form is perceptible.
Op. 31 has its two subjects in tonic minor and
relative major, though this relationship is naturally
unaltered in the repeat, and the trio proper is
immediately followed by a quasi-development of
it. And Op. 39 dispenses entirely with a trio,
the middle section consisting first of passage-
work, then of a variation of the chordal second
subject with its delicious showers of *leggierissimo*
quavers—in short, of 'development' as Chopin
understood it.

Even in the first movement of the B flat minor
Sonata the development is essentially an improvisation on the first subject, an agitated figure admir-
ably adapted to this wild hunt through a thicket of
keys. In other respects, the movement is concise
and satisfying. The transition from the first subject
to the strongly contrasted yet somehow related
second is effected with a masterful laconicism that
reminds one of Schubert's in the corresponding

there is about as much connexion between the G minor Ballade
and Mickiewicz's grim narrative poem, with its exceedingly tough
and unpleasant hero, as between *Macbeth* and Chopin's Barcarolle.
As for *Le Lac de Willis* and *Undine*, I strongly suspect that they are
one and the same poem: namely Mickiewicz's ballad, *Switezianka*,
of which a translation is given, as *The Nixie*, in *Konrad Wallenrod,
and other writings of Adam Mickiewicz*, translated by various
authors and published in 1925 by the University of California
Press. (On the other hand, by *Le Lac de Willis* Huneker may
have meant *Switéz*, which is also a poem about a haunted lake.)
Switezianka, which Rimsky-Korsakov long afterwards set as a
cantata, might conceivably have inspired the Second Ballade,
but it is absolutely preposterous to suggest that it has any
connexion with the Third.

part of the Unfinished Symphony. And the curtailment of the reprise by the omission of the first subject was inevitable; to have brought it in again after worrying it to death in the pseudo-development would have been fatal.

Yet, fine as the movement is, it is something less than first-rate Chopin. For one thing, the whole piece consists of unmodified four- or eight-bar phrases (only the very last bar is thrown in as an extra) and such undisguised squareness of phrasing sustained for such a long period is unusual with Chopin. Symmetrical phrasing is the rule rather than the exception in the études, where it often usefully holds together what might easily have become an amorphous play of motives, and it inevitably predominates in the dance-forms and in the song-like nocturnes. But, especially in the latter, Chopin usually takes considerable pains to conceal the fact. Consider, for instance, how in the opening of the A flat Nocturne, Op. 32, No. 2, he evades the seemingly unavoidable squareness of a sustained B flat in the fourth bar of the main melody, extending it ornamentally instead and then gliding imperceptibly into the repeat. He adopts exactly the same procedure at the equivalent points in the D flat Prelude and the Nocturnes, Op. 27, No. 1, and Op. 37, No. 1, to name only three of the most obvious cases. And he has at his command a score of other devices for the same purpose. The *cantabile* melody of the Fantaisie-Impromptu, for instance, just contrives to avoid banality by the premature entry of the second

four-bar clause, half a bar too soon—an example of
what it is tempting to call '*rubato* of phrase
conception'.

The same principle is often carried further, as
in the middle section of the C sharp minor
Polonaise, Op. 26, No. 1, where Chopin cuts across
the 3/4 rhythm with a motive that suggests a
contraction to 2/4, and then inserts a penultimate
compensating bar:

Ex. 22

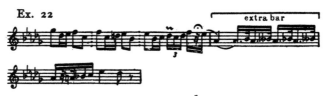

As Leichtentritt points out, the passage is a genius's
version of what a mediocrity would have written as:

Ex. 23

Much of the capricious charm of Chopin's music
is due to similar irregularities of phrasing or to the
persistent use of unusual phrase-lengths, such as
the six-bar units of the Mazurka, Op. 24, No. 3.
He was a perfect master of the arts of phrase-
overlapping, phrase-extension, and phrase-contrac-
tion. In at least one delightful instance, the end of
the Mazurka in A flat, Op. 41, No. 4, a phrase is
not merely contracted but deftly cut short. We hear

only six of the anticipated eight bars and are neatly dropped into a silence as unexpected as that which terminates Act I of *Pelléas et Mélisande*. Chopin here does rhythmically what Debussy more than half a century later did harmonically. At the end of the E flat minor Étude, Op. 10, No. 6, on the other hand, he produces a charming effect with a thirteen-bar phrase produced by the insertion of five additional bars before the final chord.

Chopin's phrase-extensions are specially interesting, for their very nature is often peculiarly conditioned by the type of melody. Two examples must suffice: from the Mazurka in B minor, Op. 33, No. 4, and from the Nocturne in F, Op. 15, No. 1. The predominance of motive-generated melody in the mazurkas has already been mentioned; in this particular mazurka the first eight-bar phrase is extended to twelve bars by a process of generation from the melodic cell A-C sharp:

Ex. 24

extension

A similar but less subtle play with a final motive is responsible for bars 21–2 of the same piece. In the Nocturne the melody is purely lyrical and the structural extension, the long yet uncompleted phrase that concludes the first part of the piece, arises from an essentially lyrical impulse to expansion. The effect is heightened by the irregular

grouping of the clauses (5 + 3 bars) coming after a
series of four-bar units.

Despite these numerous exceptions, of course,
the four-bar or eight-bar phrase remains the
foundation of Chopin's melody; the regularity is as
essential to the charm of the irregularities as firm
tempo is to the charm of tempo rubato. The metrical regularity is far less often broken than skilfully
concealed. In this as in practically every other
aspect of his melody, Chopin never completely
shook off the two great primary influences that
formed it: the contemporary Italian opera aria and
the Polish folk-dance tune.

That Chopin's melody is heavily indebted to
Bellini's is a commonplace of criticism. One has
only to open at random the score of, say, *I Capuletti
e i Montecchi* (produced in 1830), to be confronted
with a melody that might easily belong to a Chopin
nocturne:

Ex. 25

But the debt is not to Bellini only.[1] It is significant that as early as 1825 Chopin wrote 'a new polonaise on the *Barber*' (now lost) (letter of November, 1825), and the following year based the trio of a Polonaise in B flat minor on an air from *La gazza ladra*, that the Tarantelle of 1841 is obviously indebted to Rossini's, that Chopin could accompany from memory the once celebrated tenor, Franz Wild, in an air from Rossini's *Otello*. Nor did Chopin absorb all his Italianism directly. There can be little doubt that some of it was acquired at second-hand **through** Elsner and through his admired Spohr. Spohr's violin cantilena was admittedly based on Italian song and, as Dr. Maria Ottich points out,[2] 'does not consist merely of melody concealed by delicate tendrils of ornamentation but forms a self-contained line in which there is not a single merely decorative note'. Even the peculiar romantic *morbidezza* characteristic of Bellini and Chopin is common also to Spohr.

Still, it was the voice rather than the violin that Chopin admired, and it is even possible to detect in

Ex. 26

---

[1] Nor is the indebtedness all on one side. If Chopin owed much to his friend's melody, Bellini was not uninfluenced by the other's harmony. This is particularly noticeable in his *Puritani* (1835); see, for instance, Elvira's aria in Act II at the words 'Qui il giurava e poi crudele', and the remarkable chain of dominant sevenths in the duet in Act III.

[2] *Chopins Klavierornamentik*. Berlin. 1938.

his melodies purely vocal mannerisms, such as this
effect of breath-taking in the E flat Nocturne (Ex. 26),
which has dozens of parallels, many of them actually
marked by brief rests (see Ex. 28*a*, end of bar 3).

All the same it would be a disastrous mistake to
regard the melodies of the nocturnes and Chopin's
nocturne-like melodies in general as mere echoes
or imitations of Italian song-melody. As I have
said elsewhere,[1] Chopin had 'an instinct amounting
to genius for inventing melodies that would be
actually ineffective if sung or played on an instrument capable of sustaining tone but which, picked
out in percussive points of sound each beginning
to die as soon as born, are enchanting and give an
illusion of a singing that is often lovelier than
singing itself'. In other words, Chopin's melody,
in so far as it is Italian, is not an imitation but a
stylisation of Italian *bel canto*.

To take only one example of his method: he
produces marvellous pseudo-cantabile effects by
repeating a note instead of sustaining it. (See the
opening of the B flat minor Nocturne, Op. 9, No. 1,
for one of hundreds of cases, bar 11 of the *sostenuto*
section of the First Impromptu for a slightly more
subtle example of melodic intensification by this
means.) The device is in the direct line of descent
from the *vibrato* and *Bebung* of the clavichordists;
Mozart and Beethoven did not overlook it; but
Chopin's peculiar application of it to this particular
type of melody owes less to the practice of these
great predecessors than to that of John Field (cf.

[1] *A Hundred Years of Music.* Duckworth. 1938.

the opening of the latter's Nocturne No. 2 in C minor). And we must not overlook the fact that the Italian opera-composers themselves employed both *parlando* effects—'speaking' on a single note— and coloratura note-repetition.

Not only do the melodies themselves remind one of Italian opera. Their treatment—the too seductive thirds and sixths of the D flat Nocturne, the Mazurka, Op. 17, No. 1, and a dozen other works —often seems to have been suggested by the same models. Chantavoine[1] even contends that Chopin based his famous *tempo rubato* on the practice of 'the tenors and sopranos of the Italian Opera who compelled the conductor to respect their "good notes"' and all the rest of the virtuoso singer's stock-in-trade. It is certainly true that the invention of *tempo rubato* has been attributed to an Italian singer-composer, F. A. M. Pistocchi (1659– 1726),[2] but the practice was well known not only to the Italians but to Mozart and other South German composers of the eighteenth century, and (more to the point) was employed by Chopin's own master, Elsner, and other Polish composers.

Chantavoine is probably on safer ground when he suggests that Chopin's melodic ornamentation 'does not so much resemble the cadenzas of the classics and the fioriture of the German pianists— Moscheles, Hummel and the rest—as the vocal

[1] In the essay, 'L'Italienisme de Chopin', in *Musiciens et poètes* (Paris, 1912).

[2] See Lucjan Kamieński's essay, 'Zum tempo rubato', in the *Archiv für Musikwissenschaft*, I, 1.

fireworks of the virtuosi of *bel canto*'. Hummel is
not so easily dismissed as that. Musical genealogy
is seldom even as simple as Solomon's little
problem; any element in any composer may have
as many as half a dozen parents, and Hummel's
fioriture make him liable to one of the several
affiliation orders that might be issued in respect of
Chopin's. Nevertheless, the influence of vocal
coloratura, perceptible in Field too, is unmistakable
in Chopin from the *larghetto* of the F minor Concerto to the B major Nocturne, Op. 62, No. 1—
though admittedly the patch of coloratura in the
latter is exceptional in the later works.

But Chopin's is exquisitely stylized coloratura,
not a mere imitation such as some of his predecessors had been content with—for, of course, he
was not the first piano composer to take hints from
the opera stage. 'Hitherto this species of adornment
had only been modelled on the fioriture of the grand
old school of Italian song', says Liszt.[1] 'Embellish-
ments for the voice, although they had become
stereotyped and had grown monotonous, had been
servilely copied by the pianoforte; Chopin endowed
them with a charm of novelty, surprise, and variety,
quite unsuitable for the singer but in perfect
keeping with the character of the instrument.'

Yet if Chopin stylized the methods of singers he
studied them at first hand and, like C. P. E. Bach
in his *Versuch über die wahre Art das Clavier zu
spielen*, demanded that his pupils should do the

[1] *Life of Chopin*. (John Broadhouse's translation.) William
Reeves, n.d.

same. And it is significant that he particularly
admired fine coloratura. We find him praising
Sabine Heinefetter for her 'coloratura like so many
pearls', and 'enchanted' with Henriette Sonntag:
'Her *diminuendo* is the *non plus ultra* that can be
heard; her *portamento* wonderfully fine; her chromatic scales especially toward the upper part of
her voice unrivalled[1]. . . . She uses a few embroid-
eries of a quite new type.' And he preferred
Damoreau-Cinti to Malibran on the ground that
'the latter astonishes one, but Cinti charms. She
sings the chromatic scales and coloratura almost
more perfectly than the famous flute-player Tulou
plays them'. The influence of pearly chromatic
vocal coloratura is very obvious in many passages
of Chopin (e.g. the Nocturne, Op. 9, No. 1, bar 3)
and Dr. Ottich is surely right in regarding such
effects as:

Ex. 27

(a) Nocturne, Op.9, No.3

(b) Nocturne, Op.15, No.2

[1] According to Niecks's translation. That by E. L. Voynich
(*Chopin's Letters*. Desmond Harmsworth. 1932) is materially
different: 'Especially her ascending chromatic scales are exquisite.'

as stylized *portamento*. Pianists would do well to
bear that in mind.

On the other hand the quasi-recitative element in
Chopin's melody—e.g. the left-hand octave passage
in the C sharp minor Nocturne, or the end of the
B major, Op. 32, No. 1—often seems to owe as
little to the recitatives of contemporary opera as to
the earlier instrumental recitatives of C. P. E.
Bach and others. Recitative-like in intention and
effect, these passages are essentially no different
from a good deal of Chopin's purely ornamental
coloratura; for they are as much cadenza as recitative and serve the same purpose of breaking the
regular metrical pattern. One cannot imagine
them with words fitted to them, as one can some of
Liszt's instrumental recitatives.

Despite the enormous importance of chromaticism in Chopin's music, his melody is predomi-
nantly diatonic. In the vast majority of cases the
chromatic elements in it are unessential and purely
decorative: passing notes, parts of ornaments, and
so on. (As we shall see presently, that is also true to
a great extent of Chopin's harmony.) One is
reminded of Abert's remark on 'the peculiar fusion
of diatonicism and chromaticism in Mozart's piano
style'.[1] 'Despite the intermingling of chromatic
elements, the ground-structure of his melody is
diatonic. . . . And the chromaticism serves far more
often to smoothe off than to sharpen melodic con-
tours.' That is almost equally true of Chopin,
though there are a good many cases where he uses

[1] *W. A. Mozart.* Two volumes. Leipzig. 1924.

that typical nineteenth-century device of 'chromatic alteration', which has been aptly compared
with the *musica ficta* of the Middle Ages, to intensify
melodic as well as harmonic expression. The D
natural in bar 5 of the C sharp minor Nocturne
may be explained harmonically, but that at bar 13 is
a different matter; the harmony calls for D sharp
and the unexpected flattening is an intensification—
which the composer has underlined with an accent
mark. The melody strains down, as it were, toward
the C sharp that follows; the leading-note principle
here makes itself felt in the 'downward sharpening'
(which we are paradoxically obliged to call flattening) of the second degree of the scale, just as
centuries before it had made itself felt in the
sharpening of the seventh degree of the modes.
The same thing happens in bar 3 of the F sharp
Nocturne, Op. 15, No. 2, which is a repetition
doubly intensified: by the quintuplet replacing
the group of four semiquavers in bar 1, and by
the chromatic alteration of the fourth note of the
quintuplet (in this case the sixth degree of the
scale). On the other hand, the F double sharp in
the melody of bar 5 is obviously conditioned by
the harmony.

The sharpened fourths that occur so frequently
in the mazurkas are another matter. As already
explained, they are not 'alterations' at all but
normal features of a scale commonly used in Polish
folk music.

Polish elements also play a part in that rich
ornamentation which is so peculiarly characteristic

of Chopin's melodic style. The grace-notes and
interpolated triplets characteristic of the folk mazurka, for instance, crop up continually not only in
the mazurkas and polonaises, where one expects
to find them, but in the valses (cf. Op. 69, No. 1,
bars 1 and 3) and even in Chopin's most Italianate
melodies (cf. the Nocturnes in D flat, Op. 27, No.
2, bars 11–13, 16, 21, etc., and A flat, Op. 32,
No. 2, bar 9).

Arabesque melodic ornamentation in general is
such an integral part of Chopin's music that one is
tempted to propound the riddle, 'When is ornamentation not ornamentation?'—to which, of course,
the answer is 'When it is Chopin's'. It may not
be true of his early works, but his later compositions
(the last most of all) confront us with the paradox
of 'ornamentation' that constitutes the very substance of the thing ornamented. Even the straight-
forward scale and arpeggio passage-work of the
classics is everywhere replaced by free arabesque
lines.

Chopin inherited from his predecessors, from
the harpsichord and clavichord composers and
C. P. E. Bach to Mozart, Field, and Hummel, a
rich collection of stereotyped ornaments—trills and
chains of trills, *acciaccature*, turns, mordents, and
the rest—all of which he drew on freely throughout
his career.[1] And in common with his virtuoso

[1] In his mature works Chopin uses even these in an individual
way. Note how he employs turns and inverted turns to emphasize
repeated notes in the melodies of the D flat Prelude, the G minor
Nocturne, Op. 37, No. 1, etc. There are classical precedents, yet

contemporaries—Thalberg and the rest—he enriched them by employing them, particularly the
trill, in thirds and sixths. (In one third-period work,
the in every way remarkable Polonaise-Fantaisie,
he even wrote a three-part trill in thirds and sixths
simultaneously.) These older forms of ornamentation are introduced most abundantly, perhaps
superabundantly, in the earlier works: first, purely
and simply as external decoration, then, even
as early as the *Là ci darem* Variations and still
more in the concertos, as expressions of creative
exuberance.

With the concertos, however, at the same time
Chopin begins to use ornamentation in the quite
different, far more poetic spirit characteristic of his
maturity. Like melodic chromaticism, one of its
main functions is to veil and soften outlines that
would otherwise be too clear and obvious—too
classical. Coloratura decoration conceals the most
commonplace harmonic cadences (Impromptu in A
flat, bar 14 of the *sostenuto* middle section); less
florid ornamentation serves to disguise note-
repetition (Nocturne Op. 32, No. 2, bar 6). With
Chopin ornamentation commonly takes the place
of true variation, particularly in his less mature
compositions. He is particularly fond of immediately repeating a simple *cantabile* phrase in a florid
form:

in the classics such intensifying ornaments might be removed
without very serious damage to the melody—they are, after all,
only ornaments—whereas in Chopin they are indispensable parts
of the melodic line.

Ex. 28

(a) Concerto, Op.21

(b) Nocturne, Op.55, No.1

Nothing could illustrate more strikingly the
evolution of Chopin's use of ornament than this
juxtaposition of the first solo theme of the F minor
Concerto with a passage from the third-period
Nocturne in the same key, written some fourteen
years later. The ornamentation in Ex. 28*a* is pure
coloratura, a typical example from the period when
the exuberance of sheer virtuosity was being trans-
muted into wealth of poetic utterance. That in
Ex. 28*b* is much more restrained, producing a
variation not unworthy of Brahms himself. The
distinction between inner substance and outward
decoration is finally obliterated; both are fused into
a new melodic line, a line which, like the instrumental lines in numerous suite and concerto movements of J. S. Bach and other composers of the
baroque period, is as much significant 'passage' as
melody in the everyday sense.

'Significant line', something between melody
and passage-work, but originating in embroidery
of a harmonic background, played an ever more

and more important part in Chopin's music in what I have called his third period. But there are naturally a number of instances in late second-period works. The first section of the Impromptu in A flat, the finale of the B flat minor Sonata, the F minor Etude, Op. 25, No. 2, the Preludes in B major, E flat minor, and B flat minor—practically all eve-of-third-period works, dating from 1838–9 —are symptomatic. From the familiar broken-chord technique of the Viennese classical period, Chopin here evolves infinitely more subtle effects through thinking in terms of more advanced, chromatically complicated harmony and by the free weaving in of passing notes, ornaments, and even ornaments-to-ornaments (e.g. *acciaccature* before notes that are themselves not true harmony notes). With Mozart and Hummel even the more complicated forms of broken chord, with chromatic apoggiature and other modifications, remain unmistakably harmonic and 'passage'-like. It remained for the mature Chopin to give this type of formation linear significance and thematic importance.

On the other hand, Chopin's trick of embedding a melody, as it were, in broken chords—producing what Hermann Abert has called 'singing figuration' —was mildly anticipated by Mozart (cf. the *più allegro* section of the C minor Fantasia, K. 475, and the first movement of the Concerto in the same key, K. 491). But he never used 'singing figuration' so poetically as Chopin does in the A flat Etude, Op. 25, No. 1, and the middle section of the B minor Scherzo. And the bringing out of a shadowy inner part in the upper notes of a widespread arpeggio accompaniment, as in the opening of the Étude in F minor, Op. 10, No. 9, is peculiarly Chopinesque.

It was in such details as this that Chopin improved on the superficially very similar accompaniment technique of Field. (Although Field himself was not altogether insensitive to the melodic implications of such accompaniment figures; at any rate he sometimes keeps one 'part' moving in thirds or sixths with the right-hand melody: cf. his Nocturnes No. 5 in B flat and No. 11 in E flat.) The Irish master used wide-spread left-hand arpeggios, usually in triplets, decorated them with chromatic passing notes and disposed them in more intricate shapes than the few simple formulae that had satisfied the classical writers—all of which strikingly enriched the sonority of the texture. In this respect, as in the poetic quality of his imagination, Field was emphatically superior to Hummel. But it never occurred to him to give this arpeggio accompaniment anything *more* than harmonic significance as Chopin did.

Nevertheless Chopin's debt to Field, not only in this aspect of his keyboard writing but in a score of others, was enormous.[1] Even in such a mature work as the Nocturne, Op. 32, No. 2, dating from

[1] 'Liszt's statement that the Nocturnes of Field were regarded by Chopin as "insuffisants" seems to me disproved by unexceptionable evidence', says Niecks. The weight of evidence is, indeed, all on the other side: that Chopin frankly admitted his admiration for Field's nocturnes and concertos, and constantly gave them to his pupils. But even if he had never expressed his opinion in words, it is expressed sufficiently in his own nocturnes.

1837, he was still capable of echoing the older man quite closely:

Ex. 29

(a) Field: Nocturne No 5 in B flat

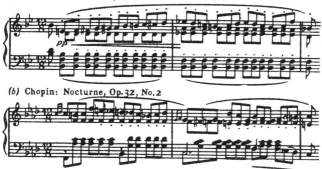

(b) Chopin: Nocturne, Op. 32, No. 2

The similarity lies not in the notes—the sort of superficial resemblance that Sir Donald Tovey has ridiculed as 'top-knottery'[1]—but in the general idea, used in each case as a contrasting middle section in a purely cantabile piece.

The author of the article 'Pianoforte-Playing' in *Grove*, however, draws attention to an important difference between Field's piano-writing and Chopin's: 'the passages of embroidery in which both delight require, in Field's case, that perfect equality of finger at which the earlier writers aimed; in Chopin the essential weakness of the human hand is turned to beautiful account, for his passages are

[1] See *Essays in Musical Analysis,* Vol. i. Essay on Haydn's Symphony No. 88, in G.

often devised in such a manner that the weak finger of the hand has to play the note which is to be comparatively unimportant. In the concertos and studies the natural conformation of the hand is kept before the composer's eye, and, as a consequence, his difficulties are always of a kind that is grateful to the player, however intricate they may sound.' This principle of turning to account the inherent limitations of the human hand was carried still farther by Liszt.

And if Chopin learned from Field everything that the latter could teach·him, he invented dozens of keyboard effects the older composer had never thought of: hazy, almost impressionistic pedal effects, contrasts of scoring both subtle (Étude in E, Op. 10, No. 3, bars 15–18) and striking (the D flat subject of the Third Scherzo, with its delicious *leggierissimo* showers of quavers interspersed among the *sostenuto* chord passages), left-hand bravura (Étude in C sharp minor, Op. 25, No. 7), persistent cross-rhythms (two of the Trois Nouvelles Études). Indeed he possessed a fertility in the invention of pianistic devices so inexhaustible that, a few favourite formulae apart, hardly any two pieces seem to be laid out in the same way.

In all this, of course, one sees the exuberance of the virtuoso working with absolute ease in his own peculiar medium. If the inspiration did not actually come first from the fingers, at least it must have come from fingers and brain simultaneously working in closest collaboration. It is impossible to hear such pieces as the Preludes in F sharp minor

and F major, and not to realize the creative impulse
that Chopin drew from the very feeling of his hands
on the keyboard—the keyboard, be it remembered,
not of our modern concert grand with its heavy
touch and iron resonance, but of the old-fashioned
'square' piano with its simpler mechanism, lighter
touch, and thinner tone.

There can be little doubt, I think, that Chopin's
harmony—the most important, most individual, and
most fascinating of all aspects of his music—was
also largely inspired, or at any rate discovered,
in the same way: by improvisation at the keyboard.
There may have been precedents for some of his
harmonic exploits, notably in Spohr, but it is
obvious that many of them were directly inspired
by the timbre of the instrument or brought to light
by the improviser's delicate fingers. And this is all
the more important since even Chopin's basic
ideas are frequently harmonic rather than melodic.
The already mentioned case of the second section
of the posthumously published Valse in E minor[1]
is but one of many.

Now although the charm of Chopin's harmony
lies almost entirely in its iridescent chromaticism,
it is, like his melody, fundamentally diatonic. The
diatonic basis is usually chromatically embroidered,
frequently even temporarily broken up altogether.
But its presence is always felt. (And, of course, there
are a good many pages of Chopin as uncoloured by
chromatic harmony as a page of typical Haydn.)

The chords that form the basis of Chopin's

[1] See p. 28.

exceptionally rich harmonic vocabulary are simple
and comparatively few in number: the ordinary
diatonic triads and inversions, the major triads on
the flattened supertonic (= Neapolitan sixth)[1] and
flattened submediant, the minor form of the subdominant triad in the major mode, a favourite
chord with all the composers of the romantic
period (e.g. in the Mazurkas, Op. 7, No. 4 and
Op. 33, Nos. 2 and 4), the dominant seventh (even
the dominant ninth is comparatively uncommon),
the diminished seventh, the added sixth (including
its minor form in the major mode), and the so-called
German sixth on both flattened sixth and flattened
second degrees of the scale. The other—the
'French'—form of augmented sixth is rather rare
in Chopin: he uses it for the peak chord at the end
of the F major Ballade, as if feeling it to be
peculiarly intense. Secondary sevenths and ninths
seldom or never occur, unless we consider the added
sixth an inversion of a secondary seventh. The
secondary ninth twelve bars before the end of the
A flat Ballade, a third-period work, is quite
exceptional.[2]

[1] I must remind the reader that in speaking of chords I have in
most cases not differentiated between inversions and root-positions,
as the tonal functions are usually the same whatever the inversion.

[2] The numerous chords foreign to the key with which Chopin's
music is liberally sown may be understood in the light of the
German theory of interdominants (*Zwischendominanten*), which
will be explained later, better than in the twilight of the lamentably
misnamed Dr. Day's theory of supertonic and tonic 'fundamental
discords' which has cursed English harmony-teaching since the
middle of the last century.

But Chopin often overlays these simple basic chords with appoggiaturas, suspensions, anticipations, and passing notes so richly that, especially in his later works, they are almost unrecognizable. And analysis of his harmony is by no means simplified by his habits of presenting progressions in the sketchiest of skeleton forms, as in the already mentioned modulation in the F sharp Impromptu,[1] the opening of the C sharp minor Scherzo, and the finale of the B flat minor Sonata, and of writing in convenient rather than grammatically correct notation.

Even in such comparatively early works as the E flat Nocturne and the 'Black Key' Étude we find Chopin using suspensions and passing notes with characteristic freedom. In the second half of the very first bar of the Nocturne a suspension (F in the right hand) and a passing note (D in the bass) combine to prevent the E flat chord from being heard at all in its pure form. And the Étude contains striking examples of the effects a genius can wring from a single chord sustained for four bars (25–8) with diatonic passing notes in the treble and chromatic passing notes in the bass, and, five bars later, from a suspension (the D flat) held for four bars—or rather scattered over three octaves for four bars—implied in the fifth and resolved only in the sixth. The distribution of the suspended note by figuration is, of course, thoroughly characteristic of Chopin. Writing for the keyboard with its partial obliteration of true part-writing, he

[1] See p. 54.

felt perfectly free to resolve dissonant notes in 'wrong' parts or to introduce passing notes in parts other than those to which they rightly belong.

Of the innumerable beautiful or powerful transition chords (or pseudo-chords) produced by suspensions or passing notes, two examples must suffice:

Ex. 30

(a) Nocturne, Op.15, No.1

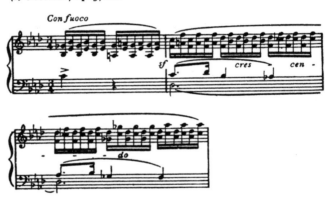

(b) Nocturne, Op.27, No.1

The faint clash of the suspended C and A natural
in the second bar of Ex. 30*a* is as delicious as the
G flat passing notes in the third. (It will be noticed
that the true harmony does not change at all in bar
3.) In Ex. 30*b* the chromatic passing note produces
a pseudo-chord of great intensity.

From this it was but a step to the use of such
formations as chords in their own right, omitting
the 'true' note altogether: the introduction in harmony of the same principle of chromatic alteration
which we have already observed in Chopin's melody,
and which was ultimately to lead nineteenth-
century harmony through *Tristan* to the Schönberg
of the *Klavierstücke*, Op. 11. Indeed the so-called
'French sixth' on the flattened supertonic, which
Chopin himself used from time to time (e.g.
Prelude in C minor, bar 6, and Polonaise in A,
eighteen bars before the end of the middle section),
is really the dominant seventh (second inversion)
with the fifth chromatically altered.

This multiplication of appoggiaturas, passing
notes, suspensions, and anticipations, usually in
chromatic forms, produces an extraordinary plas-
ticity, even fluidity, in the harmonic substance, so
that at times *all* the parts are found to be moving
by semitones as in *Tristan*. Transitional passages
produced simply by semitonal movement of parts
are very common in Chopin. Sometimes the movement is quite obvious, as in the E minor Prelude,
the opening bars of the B flat minor Sonata and the
Mazurka in the same key, Op. 24, No. 4, the
Mazurka, Op. 17, No. 2 (end of middle section);

sometimes exquisitely concealed by the keyboard lay-out, as in the D flat Nocturne, Op. 27, No. 2 (bars 42–5). And Chopin uses the same technical device for very different aesthetic purposes: in the Sonata and the B flat minor Mazurka to conceal the tonic key and enhance the effect of its appearance when it does come,[1] in the E minor Mazurka to modulate, in the Prelude to suggest profound and deepening gloom, in the Nocturne to add a new range of shimmering harmonic colours to the already rich key of D flat.

The last example is perhaps the most characteristic and the most important. Any bungler could have seen what possibilities the device offers for easy modulation. Hundreds of extemporizing organists have done so, if with something less than Chopin's skill. Spohr had discovered its uses as a means of extending a key or even temporarily obliterating tonality. But it remained for Chopin to use it in this sense with consummate artistry, subtly disguising it, avoiding the dangers of its merely meandering tendency, giving it purpose and direction, and drawing from it its maximum possibilities of colour.

Perhaps another and more virile example, taken from the Étude, Op. 10, No. 8, will make this clearer:

---

[1] There is a Mozartian precedent just before the reprise in the first movement of the E flat Piano Concerto, K. 449.

Ex. 31

It will be seen that this apparently fairly complicated progression really consists of this very simple one:

Ex. 32

—that in fact there is no modulation at all. The music proceeds from one inversion of the dominant seventh to another simply by semitonal movement of parts, the intervening chords being purely transitional and having no tonal function. The

chord at bar 4 is neither the dominant seventh of E
flat it appears to be nor even a German sixth in D
minor written enharmonically, but simply an
accidental transition form. (There are dozens of
similar cases in Chopin; for instance, the chord in
the second bar of Ex. 21.) The whole of Ex. 31,
then, is not a modulation but an extension of D
minor, 'an iridescent play of colour, an effect of
superficies, not an effect of substance', as Hadow
said of the similar but much briefer and more
delicate passage in the E flat Nocturne.[1] At the
same time it is obvious that its D minor-ness is
determined only by its first and last chords;
removed from its context, the passage would be
completely atonal.

It will be noticed that no fewer than three of the
transition chords in Ex. 31 take the form of
diminished sevenths (as do a great many of
Spohr's transition chords). Indeed the diminished
seventh plays an extraordinarily important part in
the undermining of tonality not only in Spohr and
Chopin but in their immediate successors, Liszt
and Wagner.

We have already noticed the semitonal side-slip
of diminished sevenths in Chopin's early works
(see Ex. 9), ornamental passages temporarily
breaking up the tonal surface. Naturally this idea is
elaborated in more mature compositions. Sometimes it remains decorative, if more skilfully laid
out, as in the middle section of the E major Étude,
Op. 10, No. 3. But already in another of the Op.

[1] See p. vii.

10 Etudes (No. 1 in C) this progression ceases to be mere glittering decoration and becomes colourful, non-tonal substance (bars 8–6 before the end). As such, it lends itself equally to exquisite melting effects, as in the Nocturne in D flat, Op. 27, No. 2, bars 62–4 and 66–8, where the tonic pedal prevents its losing its tonal bearings, and to the expression of intense excitement, as in the peroration of the F major Ballade. In the B flat minor Scherzo (bars 17–22 of the final *Più mosso*) it is used in exactly the same sense as in the Ballade, but intensified by appoggiaturas. In the Mazurka, Op. 7, No. 2, the succession of sevenths is further disguised by suspensions producing intermediate transition chords:

Ex. 33

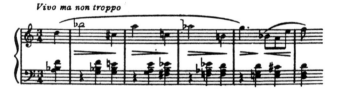

a passage as entirely in Chopinesque D minor as Ex. 31.

From semitonal progressions of diminished sevenths it was only a step to freer progressions, e.g. in alternate whole tones and semitones as in the Nocturne, Op. 15, No. 3, at the beginning of the transition to the second section. And from the chromatic side-slipping of diminished sevenths only another step to the chromatic side-slipping of

dominant sevenths; Chopin takes it in the C sharp
minor Scherzo, the Mazurka in the same key, Op.
30, No. 4 (a curiously Debussyesque passage), the
A flat Nocturne, Op. 32, No. 2, and other works.
The two following examples are specially characteristic of Chopin's appoggiatura and figuration technique, and of his love of piquant sound-clashes:

Ex. 34

(a) **Prelude, Op.28, No.8**

Molto agitato

(b) **Etude in D flat (from 'Trois Nouvelles Etudes')**

Allegretto

Chopin is equally fond of another type of
dominant-seventh series, quite different in origin
(being essentially a chain of interrupted cadences),
in which the root of each chord is a fifth lower than
its predecessor. In other words, each chord
resolves on the expected triad, plus an extra minor
third producing a new dominant seventh. There

are numerous examples in Chopin's work. Thus in the Étude, Op. 10, No. 1 (bars 24–35), he leaps from a dominant chord in A through a series of dominant sevenths (disguised by suspensions and appoggiaturas) in D, G, C, F, and B flat to E flat. The F in the last chord is then flattened, producing enharmonically a French sixth (altered form of dominant seventh) in A. The A major triad appears in the next bar, after a ten-bar parenthesis. At the end of the C sharp minor Étude, Op. 25, No. 7, a much 'tighter' chain of sevenths is given a characteristic twist at the end, producing a brief parenthetic emphasis on the key of the dominant before dropping back into the tonic:

Ex. 35

The first chord of the second bar, instead of the anticipated dominant seventh in A, is merely a transition form (the D sharp being suspended instead of resolving on to D natural) leading to the minor form of the added sixth in G sharp. But the next chord, the dominant seventh in G sharp, resolves on to an added sixth in C sharp minor— and we are home again. We thus get a sort of full close raised to the second power.

Other interesting examples of such chains of sevenths will be found in the Polonaise, Op. 26, No. 1 (bars 13–14 of the *meno mosso* section), and in the Mazurkas, Op. 6, Nos. 1 (bars 5–9) and 3 (bars 27–8 of the middle section). In the two latter cases the chain is characteristically disguised by passing notes producing transition chords. In the Mazurka, Op. 17, No. 1, the chain is dislocated in the middle by a foreign chord, D–F–C–A flat, taken as a chromatically altered form of the chord on D flat and left as an altered form of the chord on D natural. But the dislocation is characteristic of Chopin. If he has mannerisms, he never actually repeats himself; some new disguise, some unexpected twist always gives freshness and vitality to what might otherwise have degenerated into mere formula.

These chains of dominant sevenths are, as I have said, elaborations of the interrupted cadence. Extremely lavish employment of interrupted cadences is one of the most important symptoms of romantic harmony in general and Wagner's in particular, and Chopin also anticipates Wagner in other favourite forms of it, such as resolution on a chord with root a third lower than the expected one (e.g. Scherzo in B flat minor: bar 49 of the working-out section). Again, the dramatic interrupted cadence near the end of the Nocturne, Op. 32, No. 1, is extraordinarily Wagnerian.

These series of diminished and dominant sevenths show how much importance Chopin attached to harmonic progressions for their own sake, to what we may call the *absolute* value of such progressions. It was only to be expected therefore that he should have made very free use of series of absolute progressions: in other words, of harmonic sequences. Here again, quite as much as in his interrupted cadences and his free use of chromatic appoggiaturas and passing notes, Chopin was one of the direct precursors of Wagner. (He in turn, of course, must have been familiar with numerous precedents in earlier masters, above all in Beethoven.) And here, too, although he works the basic idea almost to death, his disguises and modifications of it are infinitely varied.

The harmonic sequence by whole tones, whether rising or falling, is the general rule with Chopin, that by semitones in the A flat Prelude (bars 51–3) being quite exceptional. A very simple, yet typical instance of harmonic sequence by whole tones occurs in the D major middle section of the Polonaise in A, Op. 40, No. 1. A cadence in the dominant is followed by a German sixth also in A major; this is taken in the sense of a dominant seventh in B flat and initiates a sequence of full closes in B flat, C, and D. The whole passage is yet another example of key-extension; there has been no real modulation at all. One suspects it was such passages as this which provoked the remark of Moscheles about 'the harsh modulations which strike me disagreeably when I am playing Chopin's compositions' and which annoyed more conservative contemporaries still more deeply.

Naturally Chopin's harmonic sequences are not

always simply extensions of a key. They are also a very common means of modulation, though seldom employed crudely without some touch of ingenuity at the crucial point of arrival in the new key: a dominant seventh-German sixth or other enharmonic pun, a chromatic alteration turning a dominant into a diminished seventh or vice versa, in one case (the Étude, Op. 10, No. 4, bars 41–4) a dissolution into a shower of diminished sevenths before crystallization into the new key. Once again it cannot be too strongly emphasized that if Chopin had favourite devices he never, or very seldom, lapsed into routine. The more clearly one recognizes his basic formulae, the greater is one's delight in his variations of them. He sometimes repeats one or more members of a sequence (e.g. the G minor Ballade, bars 16–13 before the reprise); in the Mazurka, Op. 24, No. 3, he not only repeats one member but carries the harmonic sequence across the beat, just as he carries the melody across the beat in the Valse, Op. 42, and the E major Scherzo.

Like the side-slipped-diminished-seventh device, the harmonic sequence is used in Chopin's hands for very different aesthetic purposes: for effects of the most delicate poetry (Nocturne, Op. 37, No. 2, bars 25–7) and for powerful effects of glowing climax, as in the F major Ballade (bars 17–22 of the first *Presto*: a passage standing midway between the development section in the Adagio of Beethoven's *Hammerklavier* Sonata and the sequence technique of Liszt and Wagner).

Somewhat akin in feeling to the sequence are also those abrupt transitions to keys a tone, a semitone, or a third away which one finds so frequently in Chopin and other romantic composers. It is true there were precedents in the classics for these juxtapositions of distant keys. 'Mediant key-relationship' can be found not only in late Haydn and in the *Emperor* Concerto but in compositions of the Mannheim school. Haydn wrote a piano sonata in E flat with slow movement in E major; indeed semitonal relationship is recognized in the admission of the Neapolitan sixth and made easier by the dominant seventh-German sixth pun. But there is a vast difference between the occasional abnormal introduction of such effects and their employment on almost every page as normal parts of a composer's vocabulary. And an equally vast difference between the prosaic and the poetic.

Spohr knew all about 'tonal parenthesis'. There is a good example at the end of the Andante (a set of variations on Handel's 'Harmonious Blacksmith' theme) of his Octet, Op. 32, which Chopin heard in 1829 and thought 'lovely, exquisite':

Ex. 36

But how dry and unimaginative that sounds by comparison with these examples from two Chopin polonaises:

Ex. 37

(a) Op. 26, No. 1

(b) Op. 40, No. 2

Here in each case, as in the Spohr, the parenthesis arises from a simple enharmonic pun. But Spohr's is prose, Chopin's poetry.

We have still left untouched, however, one of the most fruitful of all sources of key-parenthesis or key-extension, one of the foundation-stones of chromatic harmony in general: the interdominant chords (*Zwischendominanten*, as German theorists call them) freely employed, not only by the Viennese classic masters, but by J. S. Bach and even earlier composers. Observing that all these masters introduced chords foreign to a key, the Father of English Harmony-Teaching, Alfred Day, tried to reduce their practice to theory by inventing a hypothetic system of tonic and supertonic discords parallel with the dominant series in each key. In so far as he recognized that chords foreign to a key do not necessarily produce even momentary modulation, Day was quite right; but in attempting to bring them into the fold by his hypothesis of supertonic and tonic 'fundamental discords'[1] he was wildly and hopelessly wrong. Even by the time his treatise was published (in 1845), it was insufficient to explain the practice of contemporary composers, notwithstanding which it provided the basis of English teaching of harmony for very many years.

For the complicated and unreal deductions of Day, it is necessary only to substitute one simple observation: that any chord in the key may be preceded by a foreign chord standing in dominant (or even subdominant) relation to it, whether dominant seventh or ninth, diminished seventh (perhaps the commonest form of interdominant), or simple triad. Thus in the B flat minor Nocturne, Op. 9, No. 1, the chords in the first halves of bars 13 and 14 are interdominants resolving on the subdominant triad and dominant seventh respectively,

[1] See p. 78.

and the second chord of bar 35, the dominant
seventh on the submediant (which Day's theory
does not account for at all), is an equally simple
interdominant to the supertonic chord in the next
bar.

The possibilities of the interdominant for key-
extension or key-parenthesis—to say nothing of
unexpected modulation—are almost unlimited.
Obviously, each interdominant chord is itself a
parenthesis within the key, or an extension of the
key on a small scale, and Chopin's music is full of
examples of interdominants introducing chains of
dominant sevenths (e.g. the Polonaise, Op. 26,
No. 1, bar 13 of the *meno mosso* section) or other
tonal digressions. The frequency of interdominants
in itself prepares the ear to accept without ques-
tion the appearance of foreign chords in a key.
Sometimes, instead of flying off at a tangent,
Chopin omits the expected resolution of the interdominant altogether; the famous penultimate bar
of the F major Prelude contains an interdominant to the subdominant triad—which is then
omitted.

As an example of colourful key-extension the
following series of interdominant chords in quick
tempo, some of them resolving on chords which
are themselves chromatic extensions of the key
(triad on the flattened sixth and major triad on
the supertonic), would be difficult to beat; it is
taken from the Étude, Op. 10, No. 7:

Ex. 38

Like the opening bars of the same Étude it is completely in C major, but in a Chopinesque C major that differs very remarkably from the C major of the Viennese classics.

Such passages in Chopin are seldom modulatory. What appear to be rapid series of modulations in his music are seldom true modulations—the first page of the G major Nocturne, Op. 37, No. 2, and the C sharp minor Prelude of 1841 are among the rare exceptions—but rather extensions of key, with consequent weakening and undermining of tonality in the classical sense, in the direction followed by Wagner, Liszt, Franck, and Schönberg. Even the Prelude to *Tristan* hardly avoids the tonic more persistently than Chopin's Prelude in the same key, Op. 28, No. 2. And both establish a subconsciousness of the tonic key by the same means: a sort of polarization in dominant and sub-dominant regions. Similarly, the opening page of the Op. 45 Prelude, after the first five bars, is surely in E major—suggested by a balance of B major against A major even more than by the later appearance of E major itself.

III

THE LAST PHASE

(1841–1849)

Tʜᴇ compositions of Chopin's last and greatest period are:

Allegro de Concert, Op. 46 (1841)
Ballades in A flat, Op. 47 (1841), and F minor, Op. 52 (1842)
Barcarolle, Op. 60 (1846)
Berceuse, Op. 57 (1843)
Fantaisie in F minor, Op. 49 (1841)
Impromptu in G flat, Op. 51 (1842)
Mazurkas, Op. 50 (1841), Op. 56 (1843), Op. 59 (1845), Op. 67, No. 4 (1846), Op. 63 (1846), Op. 67, No. 2 and Op. 68, No. 4 (1849)
Nocturnes, Op. 48 (1841), Op. 55 (1843), and Op. 62 (1846)
Polonaises, Op. 44 (1841) and Op. 53 (1842)
Polonaise-Fantaisie, Op. 61 (1846)
Prelude in C sharp minor, Op. 45 (1841)
Scherzo in E, Op. 54 (1842)
Sonata in B minor, Op. 58 (1844)
Tarantelle, Op. 43 (1841)
Valses, Op. 70, No. 2 (1842), and Op. 64 (1847)

Practically everything that has been said of the second-period works applies equally to these, too.

To analyse them in the same way and at the same length would only be to cover much of the same ground. All that remains now is to show in what way even the masterpieces of the second period are surpassed by a number of those of the third.

Anyone who knows his Chopin must be struck on reading this list of last-period compositions by the number of works to which one inevitably applies the adjective 'great': the Fourth Ballade, the F minor Fantaisie, the Mazurkas Op. 50, No. 3, and Op. 56, No. 3, both the Polonaises, the Polonaise-Fantaisie, the Nocturne, Op. 48, No. 1, and the Berceuse and Barcarolle, which are surely the two greatest of the nocturnes. It needs no analysis of style to discover that in these works Chopin entered a new, wider, and loftier sphere, acquired an almost epic breadth of conception. But analysis will show us how, while the elements of the third-period style are practically all to be found in the compositions of the second period, Chopin now not only subtilized and refined them but added a fresh element by his newly acquired grasp of counterpoint.

Harmonically the compositions of the third period are distinguished above all by their subtlety and by the accumulation and elaboration of devices already familiar. The part-writing is freer, so that we find, for instance, anticipations of notes implied but not actually sounded in the true chord that follows (e.g. the D sharp in bar 22 of the E major Scherzo). Having accustomed himself to successions of dominant sevenths a semitone apart and a

Ex. 39

(a) Impromptu, Op.51
Vivace

(b) Polonaise Fantaisie

(c) Ballade in A flat
Allegretto

(d) Mazurka, Op. 59, No. 3

Vivace

fifth apart, Chopin now writes them in whole-tone
successions, beautifully disguised by appoggiaturas, suspensions, and so on (e.g. the Mazurka,
Op. 59, No. 3, bars 65–7, and the F minor Ballade,
bars 72–5—the latter containing characteristic
examples of transition chords incidentally form-
ing diminished sevenths). Even the simplest
harmonic bases are completely overlaid with
wealth of detail. Consider these examples of
elaboration of (a) a single dominant seventh, (b) a
single diminished seventh (itself only an interdominant) over a dominant pedal, and (c and d)
side-slipped diminished sevenths. (See Ex. 39.)
Comparison of Ex. 39c with the harmonically
similar passage at the final climax of the F major
Ballade will show how Chopin had progressed in
the plastic handling of his material. Ex. 39d is a
striking anticipation of Wagner.[1]

[1] The direct influence of Chopin is apparent in a good deal of
later music, outside the main stream of Liszt and Wagner.
Drawing attention to the opening of the Mazurka, Op. 63, No. 3,
as the probable origin of melodic motives in the prologue to
Snegurochka and in Act III, Scene 2, of *Mlada*, Rimsky-Korsakov
remarked to Yastrebtsev that 'in Chopin you will find many
of the real roots of contemporary music'. (V. V. Yastrebtsev:
My Reminiscences of Rimsky-Korsakov, entry of August 30th, 1894.)

The Mazurka, Op. 56, No. 3, contains a still more remarkable premonition of a typical Wagnerian procedure: quasi-contrapuntal treatment of a theme, condensed into a given harmonic framework—in this case again a chromatic succession of diminished sevenths:

Ex. 40

Though very different from true polyphony, this passage is thoroughly typical of that breaking up of vertical harmony into horizontal thematic lines characteristic of Wagner's mature style. Just as in the seventeenth century the old fluid contrapuntal technique already began to solidify into the chordal homophony that was the rule in the last half of the eighteenth century and the first half (if not more) of the nineteenth, so in Wagner this temporarily all-predominant homophony began again gradually to dissolve into linear elements—a tendency that led eventually, through Strauss and early Schönberg (*Ein Heldenleben* and the *Gurrelieder*) to the 'linear counterpoint' of Hindemith, the polytonality of Milhaud, the canonic complications of *Pierrot Lunaire*, and the twelve-tone system. And Ex. 40 is one of the first symptoms of this tendency.

Chopin now treats non-tonal chords with even

greater freedom than before, as chords in their own right, as it were (cf. the chord at bar 5 of the Polonaise, Op. 53). Interdominants are thickly strewn in the quickest passage-work (bars 15–14 before the end of the Polonaise, Op. 44) or lead to the boldest key-extensions (e.g. in the Nocturne, Op. 55, No. 2, bars 16–13 before the end, where the interdominant principle is carried to a higher power). Tonal parenthesis becomes extremely common and even occurs in quick passage-work (e.g. the staccato quaver chords just before the coda of the F minor Ballade).

On the other hand, sequences are now frequently used on a larger scale. Instead of being treated simply as extensions of the main key, they are now used more effectively as substitutes for development, very much as Liszt used them later, and less effectively, in his symphonic poems. The development section of the A flat Ballade, for instance, ends with a modified sequence: 8 bars in B, 8 bars in C, 4 bars in D, 4 bars in E flat. The compression and consequent shortening of the later members of the sequence, and their organic overlapping, again anticipate Wagner. The development section of the F minor Ballade, though not built up of actual sequences, is constructed largely on the same principle.

Chopin's new harmonic language, carried as far as he ventured to take it, may be studied in the A flat Mazurka, Op. 59, No. 2 (bars 81–8), in the F minor Mazurka, Op. 68, No. 4, said to be his last composition, and the Polonaise-Fantaisie, bars

231–54, the most remarkable passage in a work filled from beginning to end with harmonic intimations of Wagner. The pathetically sketchy F minor Mazurka, a sort of harmonic skeleton, is a useful reminder that advanced style is not necessarily synonymous with increased aesthetic value.

The keyboard layout of the last compositions shows an advance similar to that in the harmony. On the one hand we find a refinement of the already refined; the Berceuse, for instance, quite uninteresting harmonically, is one of the supreme examples of Chopin's art of keyboard *facture*—a perfect embodiment of all the outstanding features of the new style of piano-writing: 'percussive-singing' melody, use of the pedal, chromatic filigree-work over a diatonic foundation, contrast of registers, and so on. On the other hand, one notices a new strength and additional interest supplied by the fresh contrapuntal element, presumably the belated fruit of long study of Bach's 'Forty-eight' and of more recent study of 'Cherubini's *traité*'.[1]

This new outlook is perceptible in the opening bars of the A flat Ballade, with its distribution of the principal melody over soprano, tenor, bass, and soprano successively. It leaves its marks even where one would least expect to find it: in the mazurkas— above all in Op. 50, No. 3, and in the beautiful canonic passage in the last twelve bars of Op. 63, No. 3. Indeed a tendency to canonic writing is one of the hall-marks of Chopin's third-period style (cf. the Ballade in F minor, bars 50–2, the first

[1] See p. xii.

movement of the Sonata in B minor, bars 23–8, etc.) Even when he does not employ contrapuntal devices, such as canon, Chopin betrays a strong inclination to think 'horizontally' in something like real parts instead of merely in broken up chords.

The tendency to evolve 'continuous' melodic lines through the decoration of a harmonic skeleton, already noticed in certain second-period works, now becomes more pronounced. The continuous melody of the Berceuse is something more than mere melodic ornamentation of the rocking chord basis; it has its own independent linear life, which is emphasized by the entry of the second part at bar 6. The G flat Impromptu, the latter part of the A flat Ballade, practically the whole of the F minor Ballade, a great deal of the Polonaise-Fantaisie, and the Fantaisie in F minor are rich in melodic lines 'continuous' in the Wagnerian rather than the Bachian sense, but very different from the discrete, stanzaic melodies of the earlier compositions. And, particularly in the two great F minor works, these melodic lines are often more virile, less sensuous than in the earlier Chopin. The Italian influence, as apparent as ever in the Berceuse and Barcarolle, here temporarily disappears, or is absorbed into something greater.

As we have just seen in the Berceuse, even where the Italian influence is as obvious as ever in the essential feeling, the 'continuous' tendency is often strongly pronounced. It is not only that the periods of the phrase-structure are still more skilfully disguised (compare the crucial ninth bar of

the Nocturne, Op. 55, No. 2, with the first bar) or
made more delightfully asymmetrical as in the
Barcarolle and the *Più lento* section of the C sharp
minor Valse, that the underlying harmony avoids
marked cadences in a way that anticipates Wagner
in method and often surpasses him in subtlety;
the linear feeling itself is continuous (cf. in
particular the Nocturnes, Op. 48, No. 2, Op. 55,
No. 2, and Op. 62, No. 1, the Berceuse already
mentioned, and even some of the mazurkas). The
Nocturne, Op. 55, No. 2, also illustrates the principle of motive-generated melody in continuous
cantabile form; compare bars 2, 3, and 14, and then
again bar 14 with bars 19–24.

Coloratura ornamentation persists, too, though it
appears less often. But now it is sometimes made
thematic, as it was later made by Liszt in his B
minor Sonata; the semiquaver passage in Ex. 39*b*,
for instance, grows organically, by diminution, out
of the first bar quoted.

This too is a symptom of the new quasi-
symphonic tendency apparent in the music of the
third period, a tendency manifest in the organic-
thematic tightening up of links and ornaments, in
the contrapuntal play with themes, and in a new
sweep and power in the handling of large-scale form.

In his shorter works Chopin clung to the end to
the ternary formula, though with ever greater
subtlety of modification—beginning the repeat of
the first section in the wrong key (Mazurka, Op.
59, No. 1), drastically varying it (Nocturne, Op.
48, No. 1), or both varying and shortening it

(Nocturnes, Op. 55, No. 1, and Op. 62, No. 1). In the Barcarolle the repeat of the first section includes a ten-bar quotation from the middle section.

The large-scale Mazurkas, Op. 50, No. 3, and Op. 56, Nos. 1 and 3, following the precedent of Op. 41, No. 1, described on page 49, have final development sections too important to be considered as mere codas, thus: ABA Development. (In the case of Op. 56, No. 1: ABAB'A Development, as the B section is repeated in a different key.) The F sharp minor Polonaise has not only a normal middle section but an interpolated mazurka[1]—AB Mazurka A—and the transition passage from mazurka back to polonaise is one of the finest examples of Chopin's last-period thematic workmanship. The return is made completely organic by the fusion of separate motives from the mazurka with the D–C sharp–F sharp–E sharp motive from which the whole-eight-bar introduction to the Polonaise has been built up:

Ex. 41

[1] In a letter of August, 1841, Chopin speaks of 'a new manuscript (a kind of polonaise, but it's more a fantasia)'—evidently the F sharp minor. The genre 'polonaise-fantaisie' was evidently in his mind some years before he wrote the work actually so called.

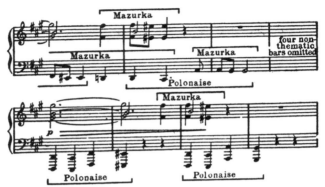

The introductory motive is then whipped up by
diminution into its original form and the main
subject of the Polonaise follows. The use of the
theme at bar 9 of the Polonaise as a bass (at bar 17
and later) and the dying-away coda are hardly less
masterly.

Still more remarkable is the Polonaise-Fantaisie,
which ranks structurally with the E major Scherzo,
the F minor Fantaisie, and the Third and Fourth
Ballades as the crown of Chopin's work. Of these
the Scherzo is the least interesting. It differs little
in plan from its predecessors, Op. 31 and Op. 39,
being laid out as follows:

Main section (two chief subjects in tonic and
        dominant)
Development
Main section (first subject only, in tonic but
        modulating to key of trio)
Trio (C sharp minor)

Main section (both subjects in original keys)
Development (as before) and Coda.

Similarly the only structural point of interest in
the first movement of the B minor Sonata is merely
a variation of a procedure in the B flat minor. This
time the reprise does not omit the whole of the
first subject, certainly, but it does skip the first
sixteen bars of it, and drastically curtails the rest, so
that, as Leichtentritt puts it, 'the broad singing
melody of the second subject appears as the real
goal of the long and complicated development'
just as in the B flat minor; though with less force
here, for it has not been excluded from the development as in the earlier Sonata.

But Chopin's conceptions of form and thematic
development were, like those of his fellow
romantics, Schumann and Berlioz, too radically
different from Beethoven's and those of the earlier
classic masters who had created the sonata, for
him to be able to cast his ideas very successfully in
this essentially classical form. While he had
progressed very far from the pitiful would-be
development of the early C minor Sonata and the
non-thematic improvisatory pseudo-developments
of the concertos, his developments—alike in the
two mature piano sonatas and in the masterpieces
we are about to discuss—are never comparable
with the great classical models. They are essentially
affairs of sequence, variation, and modulation,
swept along by powerful winds of improvisatory
inspiration and worked out with fine attention to

detail. But here again Chopin must be judged not as an inferior successor of Beethoven but as the brilliant forerunner of Liszt and Wagner.

The great Ballade in A flat follows nearly the same structural plan as the G minor, but with three principal subjects instead of two, and with the development placed *after* the reprise of the second subject:

Exposition
  A: in A flat
  B: F major and other keys
  C: A flat

Reprise: B: A flat

Development: Mostly on the B subject: various keys

Reprise
(*continued*)
  A: both in A flat and drastically
  C: curtailed

The development includes one striking symptom of Chopin's new attitude to thematic work. In the gigantic sequence through B major, C, D, and E flat with which it concludes, the theme of B is twice answered by the opening motive of A and finally fused with it into a single idea.

The form of the F minor Ballade is both simpler and more difficult to grasp. It is perhaps most easily . explained as a masterly deformation of sonata form:

Introduction: 7 bars in the dominant key
First Subject: a 73-bar working of the 4-bar theme, treated as melody, bass, in canon, and so on

Second Subject: 19 bars, in B flat; even here the
    first subject appears once in the tenor
Development: 29 bars
Reprise of Introduction, ending in cadenza (A
    major)
Reprise of First Subject: beginning in D minor
    and modulating back to the tonic; treated
    first canonically and then with 'thematic
    coloratura' variation; shortened to 34 bars
Reprise of Second Subject: in D flat, and now
    extended and treated with more breadth
Improvisatory Transition: 20 bars, leading from
    D flat to C major
Coda: F minor, with entirely fresh treatment of
    the main theme

The great Fantaisie, Op. 49, is by no means
fantasia-like in the sense of being loose or rambling
in structure. After a slow, almost symphonic
introductory march in F minor, a transitional idea
in triplets (which recurs for transitional purposes
throughout the work and again in the coda) leads
to a 75-bar passage in which four main themes
are stated in 'mediant' key-relationship: the first in
F minor, the second in A flat major, the third in C
minor, and the fourth in E flat major. The first
two subjects are then repeated in C minor and G
flat, and, with a new *lento* section in B major,
constitute the middle section of the Fantaisie. All
four subjects are then recapitulated so that their
key-sequence (B flat minor, D flat, F minor, and A
flat) now leads back to the relative major, in which

key the piece ends with a coda that includes a
reference to the *lento* theme of the middle section.

The Polonaise-Fantaisie is admittedly a harder
nut to crack. There are at least five themes, three
of which do not recur, and analysis of the form
produces only this not very illuminating result:

> Introduction: 23 bars, mainly on A:
>   various keys
> A: 42 bars; in A flat
> B: 26 bars; A flat but modulating
> A: 24 bars; A flat
> C: 32 bars; B flat but modulating

Più   ⎧ D: 33 bars; B major, etc
   lento   ⎨ E: 34 bars in G sharp minor and B
          ⎩   major—2 bars as in the Introduc-
                 tion—final 10-bar reference to E

> Transition: 16 bars
> A: 12 bars; A flat
> D: 35 bars; A flat

Yet the sequence and contrast of musical events are
perfectly satisfying and the whole piece rests solidly
on its tonal pillars of A flat. Here, in fact, we have a
free form resembling not so much the rather
square-cut symphonic poems of Liszt as the
symphonic poems of Richard Strauss written half a
century later. The resemblance is increased by
the final apotheosis of the themes I have labelled A
and D, and by the thematic polyphony of such
passages as bars 14–20 and 102–5.

Admittedly, the Polonaise-Fantaisie is, from the

point of view of form, a freakish exception in Chopin's work as a whole. But we must remember that it was one of his last compositions and that, had he lived, it might have been only the first of a new series of even bolder flights than he had taken yet. From the stylistic point of view it is his most advanced work, not only structurally but, as we have already seen, harmonically. Perhaps it is unkind to Liszt to remember that he said of it that 'although comprising thoughts which in beauty and grandeur equal—I would almost say surpass—anything Chopin has written, the work stands, on account of its pathological contents, outside the sphere of art'.

INDEX

PRINTED IN GREAT BRITAIN BY
REDWOOD PRESS LIMITED, TROWBRIDGE, WILTSHIRE